DREW L. HINDS, AUTHOR OF:

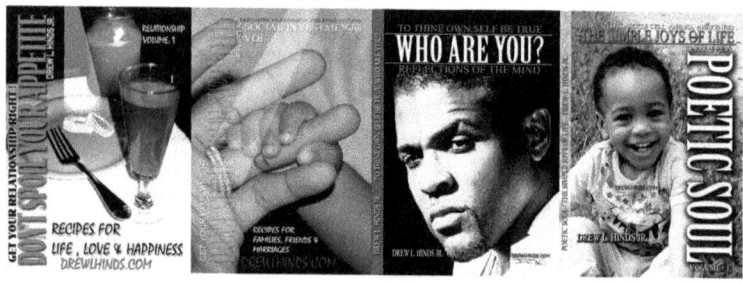

WHO ARE YOU?
POTETIC SOUL
DON'T SPOIL YOUR APPETITE (DSYA) SERIES:

VOLUME: 1 **RELATIONSHIP**: RECIPES FOR LIFE, LOVE, & HAPPINESS

VOLUME: 2 **SOCIAL INVESTMENTS**: RECIPES FOR FAMLIES, FRIENDS & MARRIAGE

"DON'T SPOIL YOUR APPETITE is a surprising delightful read. This is not just another 'RELATIONSHIP" book it is so much more. This author has mastered the craft of telling a story that grabs you from start to finish with his unique style of storytelling, poetry and some good recipes to top it off. The book explores relationships in a way that everyone can identify with. It transcends gender, genre, generations, time, and ethnicity. It really gets to what's important to you, in you and for you to be successful in any relationship.

The situations and characters may be fictional, but they were so vibrant and realistic that I was able to identify and embrace them with a sense of familiarity and truth. Truly a realistic, informative read with the right touch of wit, humor and spirituality for you to keep reading

Book Cover designed by Drew L. Hinds, Jr.
D.S.Y.A. Series managed by Vision Ink Corp.
Cover Photography by Drew L. Hinds, Jr.
(www.drewlhinds.com)
visioninkauthor@yahoo.com
Written by: Drew L. Hinds, Jr.

Edited by: Amanda Clarke & Steffi Jean-Hacques

Interviewed by: Deborah Cofer & Sheree M. Denton

Vision Ink Publishing
P.O. Box 10547
Riviera Beach, FL 33419

No part of this book may be reproduced, stored in a retrieval system, or transmitted in any form or by any means, electronic, mechanical, photocopying, recording, or otherwise without the written permission of the author.

Printed in United States of America

Copyright © 2012 Drew L. Hinds
All rights reserved.

ISBN: 0983521425
ISBN-13: 978-0983521426
Library of Congress Control Number: 2012944156

DREW L. HINDS

A GOOD MAN FOR SALE

(By His Fruits You Will Know Him)

A guide for virtuous women to know & keep Mr. Right

2012

and wanting more. I intend to purchase this book for all my male, female, single and married friends. Unequivocally one of the best books I have had the pleasure of reading in a long time. Well-done Mr. Hinds. Now that I have had a taste I am hungry for your next book and I definitely will not spoil my appetite." – A. Williams 2011 (Book Review)

This is a 2012 book review by Amanda Clarke of 'A Good Man For Sale,' prior to the release of this book:

Drew Hinds gives women an incredibly insightful look at relationships from a man's point of view in his new book, "A Good Man for Sale." He tells the truth as he sees it, and reveals both the good and bad moves women make in their relationships with men. He gives you a peak into a man's mind, and he explains why men do the things they do and how women sometimes misinterpret a man's actions.

For as far back as we can remember, men have been a mystery to women just as much as women have been a mystery to men. Drew Hinds, through this revealing book, is providing us with a chance to make a crack in the barrier that separates men and women; the barrier which prevents us from understanding each other. I definitely recommend that every woman take the time to read "A Good Man for Sale," as it may help us understand our significant other a little better, and perhaps even salvage a relationship that is in serious trouble.

As you read this book, I can guarantee that you will find a reflection of yourself in the many scenarios Drew presents us with. It may prompt you to have a moment of realization that maybe the reason your relationships are not surviving is because you do not understand men as much as you thing you do. "A Good Man for Sale" can be your guide into understanding your man's motives and needs, and perhaps even help you find that bit of comfort and happiness that you have been missing. - Amanda Clarke 2012 (Book Review)

"Men are logical beings, and if they are not happy they will become absent – whether emotionally or physically." - *DREW L. HINDS 2009*

CONTENTS

AUTHOR'S CORNER	XI
ACKNOLEDGEMENTS	
XIII	
BREAST CANCER AWARENESS	XVI
INTRODUCTION	**XVII**
TELL ME ABOUT HIM	XVIII
DEFINE A GOOD A MAN	XVIII
RETENTION PROBLEM	XVIIII
CHAPTER	
1. HE WON'T CHANGE	1
(Loving Him Unconditionally)	
WHAT IS YOUR MOTIVE?	1
PLEASE BREATH	3
POSSESSIONS	5
SPACE	6
RESPECT	7
IS IT LOVE?	8
JUST LISTEN (Poem)	9
2. I'M SURE HE KNOWS	11
(Venerability Can Equal Longevity)	
SELF-DISCLOSURE	11
TELL HIM	12
SENSUALITY	13
LOVE EXPRESSION	14
I WONDER (Poem)	16
3. REWARDING HIM	17
(Men Need Attention)	
ATTENTION	17

IT'S NOT A REWARD		18
MAKE HIM SMILE		20
GET IT TOGETHER		20
MY REWARD (Poem)		21

4. **KNOWING YOUR ROLE** ... 23
   (Knowing Why He Choose You)
   - HIS EYES ... 24
   - SUPPORT SYSTEM ... 26
   - TRUE WORTH ... 27
   - NAGGING ... 28
   - JUST FOR ME (Poem) ... 29

5. **CHOOSING HAPPINESS** ... 31
   (Men Know When They Are Unhappy)
   - GOSSIP ... 31
   - GOOD ... 32
   - BAD ... 33
   - INDIFFERENT ... 35
   - JEALOUSY ... 36
   - RELAX (Poem) ... 37

6. **BE HONEST** ... 38
   (Men Need To Know If You Are Both On The Same Page)
   - BROKEN WOMEN ... 38
   - THE PAST ... 39
   - UNEQUALLY YOKED ... 41
   - LET IT BE KNOWN ... 42
   - CAUSE & EFFECT ... 43
   - QUESTION (Poem) ... 45

7. **SECURITY CHECK** (Emotional vs. Tangible) ... 46
   - GENDER SECURITY ... 46
   - WHO MAKES THE MONEY? ... 47
   - FORGIVENESS ... 49
   - WILL HE STAY ... 50

I'M YOUR MAN (Poem)	52
8. DO YOU KNOW HIM?	53
(Knowing Of Him vs. Knowing Him)	
LET'S DANCE	53
WHO IS HE?	54
HIS THOUGHTS	57
CAN YOU IMAGINE?	58
HIS THOUGHTS	59
JUST REMARKABLE (Poem)	60
9. IF YOU DON'T, WHO WILL?	61
(You Do Know Men Have Needs-Right?)	
BACK T THE BASICS	62
STANDBY	63
REFLECTION	64
SOLUTION	65
DIVORCE	66
CHEATER	67
HIS OPTIONS	67
I NEED YOU (Poem)	68
10. NEVER COMPROMISE	70
(You Wouldn't Do It, Why Should He?)	
INTIMATE POT-LOCK	70
KNOW YOU	71
YOUR CHOICE	72
THE EXIT	73
YOUR FAITH	74
SIMPLY A PRIVILEGE (Poem)	75
FINAL WORDS	76

AUTHOR'S CORNER

"For a good man naturally works for what is good and does so for his own sake, that is, for the sake of the intellectual part of his nature, which seems to be in every man his true self."
- ARISTOTLE, Nicomachean Ethics

Drew L. Hinds served in the Army Florida National Guard for six years, and acquired an Army Achievement Medal prior to ending his tour of serves. He attended Palm Beach Community State College and pursued his Criminal Justice Undergraduate studies and is a certified law enforcement officer. Today he enjoys his time as a father, husband, mentor, author, photographer, graphic designer, lecturer, and as an operational director for Vision Ink Publishing. Drew Hinds has written and published books out his, "Don't Spoil Your Appetite/ Self Help Series." He has appeared at numerous events as guest speaker at the 2009 Harlem Book Fair in New York, the 2008 Raise the Praise Youth Convention in Toronto, On, Canada, the Riviera Beach Library Author's Night in 2010, and has been interviewed by numerous radio programs. As a police Officer he has interviewed hundreds of Domestic Violence victims and their families. He also has been featured in the compilation book, Dreams of Enchantment (The International Library of Poetry), as a member of The International Library of Poetry, and they have given him numerous awards.

Author Drew L. Hinds Jr. writes in hopes of improving the quality of life for all through character building & spiritual awareness. Mr. Hinds has been featured in the Palm Beach Post on January 5th, 2012, in the Neighborhood Post, page 4, by the title, "Riviera cop writes self-help books as therapy for violence he witnesses." He also has been interviewed by ('93 Emmy Award-Winning), News Anchor Juan Carlos Fanjul from CBS Channel 12 News, which was aired and entitled, "Self-help author 'on duty'." This young talented author needs no introduction in Palm Beach County, FL and hopes to bring more awareness to the battle against Domestic Violence, Cancer and Sickle Cell Anemia globally.

This is a 2008 interview of Drew L. Hinds by Sheree M. Denton, prior to the release of this book:

Drew L. Hinds, Jr., a driven young man whose inner being radiates passion and a deep level of insight. Within the expanse of his geographical area, he has been described as compassionate and sincere, jovial yet professional, intelligent yet modest; all being a few of the qualities that make him admirable. Drew has the aptitude to operate in the capacity of a mentor, songwriter, vocalist, freelance photographer, self-taught pianist, and author (Debut book being *Don't Spoil Your Appetite, Volume 1*).

Born to the proud parents Mr. and Mrs. Andrew L. Hinds Sr., Drew made his entry into this world in Brooklyn, New York, in the year of 1977. Unfortunately, due to the premature death of his father, Drew was deprived of those precious father-son moments, at a very early age in life. This loss proved to be the foundational element of a pivotal moment in his life, in which he culminated his relationship with the Lord; realizing that he needs Him to be his *Earthly* Father as well as his *Heavenly* Father. Drew expresses his memory of God being his "imaginary friend or daddy" at the age of two, therefore making *God* his *daddy*. The protection and consolation he receives from his "God Daddy," has given him the desire to be there for other children. In fact, Drew is affectionately called by many children "God Daddy Drew;" as he has bridged the gap, by allowing himself to be God's instrumental tool of encouragement and pure untainted love for these children. Taking up this responsibility, not having any children of his own until his recent marriage, one can say this young man surely posses the quintessence of selflessness.

"Live the dream, write the vision," is the motto that Drew lives by, and the disciplined method in which he deals with his goals. His deepest endeavor is to enlighten those who have lost hope, as he himself has been a victim of the same; recovered by the help of God and through self-motivation. Drew L. Hinds, Jr. is a driven young man whose inner being radiates passion and a deep level of insight. Within the expanse of his geographical area, he has been described as compassionate and sincere, jovial yet professional, intelligent yet modest; all being a few of the qualities that make him admirable. Drew has the aptitude to operate in the capacity of a mentor, songwriter, vocalist, freelance photographer, self-taught pianist, and author (debut book being *Don't Spoil Your Appetite, Volume 1*). In the form of vocation, Drew has served his country in the Military for eight years, where he acquired an Army Achievement Medal. Currently, he works as a police officer, in Florida, where he received a Bureau Commendation for going "above and beyond" the call of duty.
- Sheree M. Denton, 2008

ACKNOWLEDGEMENTS

"As everyone follows traditions of men, be liberated & study the origin. Knowledge is power, & I love the power you can possess." – Drew L. Hinds 2011

I am very excited that I have been moved to write yet another self-help book, and it is only by the grace of God. I would like to take the time to express my appreciation to everyone who has helped from behind the scenes, sharing their talents and inspirations with me throughout this journey.

To all my young people and godchildren, thank you for keeping me smiling, I pray that you will be blessed and highly favored in the Lord. To all my immediate family, friends, supporters and readers, I love you, and may God bless you all. My heart goes out to those who are overwhelmed by the stress of life. Trust me, God sees and knows, just have faith and know that you are never alone. This is my prayer- Speak it out loud.

"Oh Lord, if you would reach out to the broken hearted, those who are stressed and believers who have lost all hope. I pray that you would take them and free them from the bondage of their pain. Lord, I am not asking for deliverance because they are worthy but because you are merciful. Forgive us of our sins and transgressions. My heart is heavy and your people are so broken. Restore them Father; give them strength to hope again, to pray again, to sing again, to believe again, to love again, to forgive again, to confess again, to rebuke again, to stand up again, and to dream again.... Oh Lord, I know we have nothing worthy enough to offer in exchange, but we give ourselves. I pray that if there is anything amongst us that will hinder this prayer that you will remove it from our countenance, in Jesus name...Amen!"

Dedicated to:

Breast Cancer Awareness
&
All men who needed a voice and a listening ear

BREAST CANCER AWARENESS

I have found that many women are living with a disease that has gone unnoticed. Due to the lack of early detection many have lost the battle to Breast Cancer. Breast Cancer is a heterogeneous disease, which means it differs from person to person, age group, and it may also differ within the tumor itself. The disease is caused by malignant (cancer) cells from within the tissue of the breast. Each year, the ratio of women diagnosed with breast cancer versus those who die is 200,000 to 40,000. Surprisingly, the ratio of men diagnosed with breast cancer is 1,700 to 450 each year. Please - since I have lost so many friends and family to this disease, I beg of you to get tested as soon as possible; it doesn't hurt to be proactive.

INTRODUCTION

"To thine own self be true"- Shakespeare
(*Hamlet Act 1, scene 3*).

It's funny; after all these years I finally understand what Shakespeare was trying to convey with his famous quote. In fact, now I fashion my entire being around it. You see, one must truly be at peace with one's self. Only then can we recognize and fill the voids in our lives. It is not enough to just exist. Ladies, please make sure that from this moment on that you live. It should not be enough to just exist. You are worth much more than you give yourself credit. You must believe that you are much more than a degree, your worldly possessions, a well curved frame, an alluring face, or a witty conversationalist. Recover your inner peace by confessing your deepest fears and embracing your childish dreams for life, love, and the pursuit of happiness. Ladies, no matter your race, culture, or beliefs, you are my sisters and I want nothing more than for you to be happy. So, with that said, read on and accept my brotherly advise. Well that is, unless you are willing to have "A good man for sale."

I have noticed that women throughout time have revered the thought of finding, "Mr. Right." Now, don't get me wrong, that is a wonderful notion, but is finding him all that matters? Is there nothing else worth striving for other than acquiring a worthwhile man? There should be more of an emphasis on finding a 'good man,' and the reality of keeping one. I say that because far too many times there are fortunate women who find themselves involved with what they deem to be a 'good man' (better yet the right man), and yet they fail to understand the mechanics of maintaining that relationship. Now forgive me if it would seem that I am putting the responsibility entirely on a woman, because that is not the case. Yet one may come to the realization that 'good men' are truly a rare commodity.

TELL ME ABOUT HIM

So what is it that attracts you to him? Is it his physical attributes: his smile, or maybe his accent? Oh, I know…he really has a way with words. No, even better, you got a true Mandingo, that really knows how to satisfy you in more ways than one. I'm sorry, that's not it, is it? You finally found a man that accepts you for who you are, and is willing to cater to your monetary and emotional needs. Wait, don't tell me, your prayers have been answered and you have found a spiritual man, a real Boaz. Well, whatever type of man you have found that has given you contentment, congratulations!

Before I go any further, let me first explain that this book was written solely by a man for women who wish to better understand a man. So trust me, I am on your side. In fact ladies, I want you to keep this book until you truly understand how a man's mind works. Unlike our female counter parts, men rely on their animal instincts and are usually straightforward with their intentions. So ask open-ended questions and pay close attention to their response. For example, ask a question like, "What are your true intentions?" Now, if he answers 'I am not looking to get into anything serious,' translation would be: this is not his first rodeo, so he is definitely sticking and moving. Ladies, this is the point where you politely excuse yourself and run to safety.

DEFINE A GOOD MAN

Definition according to dictionary.com:
man (noun), *"1. an adult male person, as distinguished from a boy or a woman 2. a member of the species Homo sapiens or all the members of this species collectively, without regard to sex."*

good (adjective), *"morally excellent; virtuous; righteous; pious:* a good man."

I am curious to know, how you would define a 'good man' or better yet, the right man in this day and age? Would he be depicted as a provider, a heterosexual, a single man, a spiritual man, an employed man, or maybe one with no kids and good credit? Well, whatever attribute you feel may fill your void, it also should be something worth keeping. When I refer to the term a 'Good Man,' I am depicting a male that has matured to the level were he is willing and able to appreciate a Virtuous Woman. When referring to the term Virtuous Woman, I am defining a woman of worth - a wholesome woman. Both Good Men and Virtuous Women are spiritually sound individuals who have grasped the understanding that there is a higher calling for their existence. They both have acquired a giving nature and aim to improve the quality of their life, and that of others. A Good Man and a Virtuous Woman understand that a positive outlook on life is needed to maintain longevity within a meaningful relationship.

A Good Man may come in different shades and shapes but all have a common denominator: they aim to give and receive love in its entirety. A Good Man knows how to respect a woman, while acting in a leadership capacity. He values his woman's opinion, but is able to make a sound decision on his own. Media, social groups, peers or loose women do not easily misguide this man. A Good Man also is revered for putting his immediate family first and foremost in his endeavors.

RETENTION PROBLEM

I have found that some women seem to have what I call a

'*retention problem.*' Now, when I say this, I am referring to the fact that most women have acquired the basic knowledge of getting a man's attention. However, they truly lack the substance to keep him interested. Now ladies lets be real, why is it that when you meet a man you make sure you: go to the gym, get your hair and nails done regularly, constantly smell good, refrain from speaking to other men in their presence, give your undivided attention and make yourself available? As women, it comes naturally to avoid becoming too overbearing (in the beginning that is). It would seem to us men that you are naturally within your norm – not! Okay, I hear you ladies. I know men do it as well, but we will never master a women's alluring quality. In fact, I hear time after time (from men), that she is not the same woman I dated. The phony facade of being a Mary Poppins is uncouth, and the relationship will end in a bitter resolve. Trust me, men would prefer to know what they are getting themselves into. So just be yourself and allow him to fall in love with the real you.

I'm not sure if you are aware, but men are logical beings, and if they are not happy they will become absent – emotionally or physically. Yes, men on a whole will stop and admire beauty for a moment, but he truly needs substance to stick around. Proverbs 31:30 KJV says, "*Charm is deceitful and beauty is passing, but the woman who fears the Lord, she shall be praised.*" So, focus more on your *characteristics*, as oppose to superficial qualities. When I mention *characteristics* I am referring to developing a sense of selflessness, morality, dependability, self-disclosure, patience, honesty, teachable spirit, spirituality, confidence and independence. Just in case I lost you, a person with a teachable spirit is basically someone who is a good student. If you really want to preserve a relationship with a 'good man,' then learn how to be a 'good woman', as opposed to a fake one. Trust me, the rest will work itself out. That is, unless you are willing to have, "A good man for sale."

ONE

He Won't Change

Loving Him Unconditionally

"A relationship shouldn't be merely an obligation dictated by a condition, if for any reason this occurs it becomes equivalent to a job." – Drew L. Hinds 2009

WHAT IS YOUR MOTIVE?

Okay, don't look so puzzled at the subtitle... (smile). Take some time now and get something to write with. I would like you to complete a self-examination, by simply answering a few questions. Have you ever considered you're motive for seeking a man? How long did your last relationship last? Why aren't you still in your last relationship? Could you have salvaged your last relationship, if so why didn't you? Do you feel that by having a man you will be a defined woman or better yet complete? Why do you long for a man, is it some life long quest to fill a void? Do you feel pressured by society and their biological clock speech? Is there peer pressure to have kids? Do you find that you don't like being single long? Do you need a man more so for physical or mental intimacy? I believe that it is a healthy practice to re-evaluate ourselves every so often; think of it as a *'mental-enema'*.

Have you ever found yourself in a situation with a man (whom you love), and you are trying to understand why he seems so frustrated or distant? Well, that is probably why you decided to read this book – you hope to find, understand and keep a man. Before you read any further, I want you to be honest with yourself: do you need a man at this stage of your life, or is it just a want? Secondly, what kind of woman are you in relation to the man that you desire? Think about it for a moment; if you're a messy person, would it make sense to pursue a neat man? Many times we strive for unrealistic goals and wonder why our efforts have yielded a negative result. Please, be honest with yourself and spend some time alone and think about what you need, as opposed to what you want. Finally, is your present man what you need at this point in your life?

Many times I run into women who believe that a good man is the answer to all their problems. This is an unrealistic notion. You see most men are looking for a warm-hearted woman who is strong in spirit, yet light in mental baggage. Mental baggage is a term I use to describe past or present hardships, which a person finds hard to let go of. These individuals find it hard to overcome their hurt, and as a result, they subject their loved ones to bitterness. When a person is consumed by insecurities, they are constantly guarded. These individuals find it hard to self-disclose their feelings, and lack the ability to give and receive love.

I want you to understand that we have all had rough times in our lives, but we can't let these situations defeat us. Think of bad experiences as training, it can mentally strengthen as well as humble one's spirit. Never think of disappointments as a place that you are confined to. *I think a lot of people overlook the fact that if you have to think back to a situation that happened, then it is the past and you have already succeeded.* Now you just need to be grateful for getting through it and move positively towards the future. *Don't allow past experiences to hinder your present goals.* I have watched so many women lose a man they care about, and they never understood why he left. *Having that special someone in your life is a privilege, not a right.* However this can only be appreciated by a responsible and *sound adult.* I am referring to a person who is responsible, sensitive of other's feelings and is able to give and receive love unconditionally.

PLEASE BREATH

Question: Have you ever felt like your relationship was like a job that you clocked in and out of? Have you ever cringed at the thought of your significant other calling you? Have you ever daydreamed of other things you could be doing while in his presence? Have you ever found that you have nothing to talk about after a whole day of not seeing each other? Well, if your answer is yes to any of these questions, you need to stop and reevaluate your relationship.

Don't get so frustrated with a man when he seems to shy away. Usually, a man is black or white. A man will commonly tell you what is bothering him; the problem, on the other hand, is getting a woman to listen. I believe the problem begins when a woman tries to psychoanalyze a man's reasoning. For example: a man tells his lady that he has a stomachache and he is going to lie down. The woman hears his response, but understands it to mean; "I don't want to go to your mother's house so I am making up an excuse to get out of it." Well, the truth may be that you cooked your man a meal that gave him diarrhea for three days and he really doesn't want to hurt your feelings by telling you why he is feeling sick. *Stop reading into what a man says and take it at face value (until he gives you reason to think otherwise)*. Men don't think like women; for the most part we don't have hidden agendas when expressing feelings, we just say what we mean. For example, a man says to a woman: "I know we have been intimate these few weeks, but I don't want a serious relationship." A woman may hear, "I look forward to making love to you, so give me some time before I can commit." When in actuality the truth is, you made it easy for him to have sex with you, but don't think you are the only one he is being intimate with. *Don't allow your emotions to cloud your listening skills.* Word of caution, if you don't understand, then ask him to explain. Always, verbally confirm what you heard with him.

You see, if you have the right motives you will be a great partner and you won't feel the need to change him: you will compliment him. *Master the mindset that you cannot control your circumstances, but you can control how you react to them.* Only then will you be at peace. Okay, now that we have cleared the air, let's start by explaining the *mechanics of a man.* I am referring to what makes up a man's thought process. First of all, I want you to understand that men are territorial creatures. We have an innate desire to protect our own, whether it is our possessions, space or family. If a woman fails to understand that a man needs space then it can and will bring a visible distance within the relationship. Let's review these concepts.

POSSESSIONS

Let's just say that men really don't appreciate sharing what they deem to be theirs. Let me see if I can explain it in a gentler tone: *if a man has any reason to believe that something is his, then he will show some form of aggression to preserve that right.* In a man's mind, there is also a very thin line between space, tangible possessions and a significant other. For instance, I have found that there are women who find it hard to cut their losses with men from their past. I say that because I have witnessed women who have so called 'moved on,' yet they keep in contact with a past lover. In doing so, she gives off the preconceived notion that she still has mutual interest towards her past. Men don't read between lines, it is either black or white. The worst thing a women could do is be under the false pretense that, "He understands we are just friends." Now ladies, by no means am I saying that you cannot engage in platonic male friends, but just be mindful of the negative rift it can cause in a committed relationship. I have found that men, unlike women can compartmentalize (separate their emotion), from a one nightstand; yet not his need for ownership. If a man is horny, he can instinctively disengage himself from any emotional attachment (to a female), to physically fulfill his need. With that said, there are very few women (which are emotional by nature), that can be intimate with a man and go back to being just friends without an emotional attachment. So, with that said, don't sell yourself short. So, find the closest man to what you deem to be a good man, validate his intentions and marry him.

Tell me what you think about this situation: A woman decides she is attracted to a man and she gets involved. Soon after, the present male in her life notices that she receives frequent phone calls and inquires. The female assures him that all is well and that she just has a lot of friends from school that check on her from time to time. One day, while at lunch, a male approaches the couple and greets her. She introduces the male that approached the table as her friend, and all hell breaks loose. Mind you, no words were spoken to convey a verbal insult, but the nonverbal cues said it all. I for one have learned it is best for people to avoid active contact with past partners; that is if you are not attempting to destroy a new relationship. So many altercations and misunderstandings could be avoided if this simple aspect is acknowledged.

The opposite sex friendship story line doesn't go over well with men, so please stop pitching it. You have to understand that men have had sexual encounters with 'female friends,' so there is an insecurity that arises when you claim to have a platonic relationship with your old male friends. If you feel that your significant other is being unreasonable, then maybe you should let your male friend fill your void and stop pursuing a committed relationship. Whatever you decided, just remember that men are territorial.

SPACE

I am not sure why it seems so taboo (for some women), to understand that a man needs his space. Men seem to have the same territorial mindset towards space. I have heard many women get upset, due to the fact that their significant other asks for some time to hang with his friends, or wanted time alone. Women seem to have a need to plan out everything, including a man's personal time. This can be very taxing to men. *Nothing feels better (to a man) then the feeling that he made the choice to do something on his own.* It is wise to give a man his space if you want him to willingly stay involved with you. Now, keep in mind a man can be persuaded to spend time with you, but you have to allow him to come to that conclusion on his own. You can recognize a good man when he acknowledges your concerns and takes the time to reassure your emotional security. I admit there are things that both men and women do that contribute to insecurities, but it can all be resolved with good communication. Both partners openly discussing their concerns can remove insecurities.

Let me be honest, there is nothing more annoying to a man, than a woman who is always in his face. When I say in his face, I am depicting a woman constantly calling him to see where he is and not allowing him to have his space to watch his favorite television show or sporting event. These are all signs of insecurity, and a woman should work on these issues if she wishes to pursue a meaningful relationship. One has to truly be honest with one's self: if you find that you have had insecurity issues within your last few relationships, then you might want to take ownership and deal with your own inhabitations. I have heard people time and time again playing the victim role and blaming everyone else for making them insecure. Please, stop blaming others and take ownership of your own issues.

RESPECT

Yes, both men and women have personality flaws – so take a deep breath and deal with it. *We all have to face the fact that men and women are different, but it doesn't give either party the right to belittle one another.* Men, as well as women, need to feel respected, and I say that in all aspects. So be mindful of your significant other's feelings. Ask your partner if you are giving enough support. Allow your man to teach you how to cater to his needs. Be mindful, that no one knows him better than himself.

Why is it that some women feel they have to question a man's decision in public? Remember, men are logical and they rarely understand a women's outburst of emotion. This is a common problem that emasculates a man and makes him contemplate other options towards obtaining his happiness. *Yes, in a man's youth an out spoken and flamboyant girl was cute, but as time passes he matures and the confrontational aspect begins to lose its luster.* It is a matter of time before a man reveals his frustration towards a woman's overbearing and combative attitude. Now, I don't want you to be under the false pretense that a man would prefer a docile woman; but rather a pleasant one. A man understands that a woman won't always agree with him, but he finds it hard to appreciate an aggressive attitude that may come along with the response. A negative response fueled by attitude forces a male to become defensive. After a period of time he will begin to avoid conversation in hopes of evading confrontation, and then ultimately, all is lost.

IS IT LOVE?

Question: If a person says, "As long as he keeps paying my bills, I will stay committed to him," is that love? If a person's feelings can change like the wind, it would seem that it is merely conditional and not love, right? I have always believed that love (the emotion) is unconditional, a genuine and emotional bond. Why do people express that they fell out of love with their better half? Perhaps, they were merely physically attracted to their partner as opposed to having an emotional bond with them.

I see nothing wrong with being honest and realizing that you have been merely tolerating him instead of actually being in love with him. You see, once you have deciphered where your heart is; it becomes easier to move on and find true love. I have met many individuals over the years that were miserable in their relationships, yet they stayed in it. Why, you ask? Well, I would say, "The fear of loneliness." *There are people who rather stay in a stagnant, or in some cases abusive relationship to avoid being alone.* Listen, if you know that you can walk away from your present relationship and not feel remorse, then pack your bags and leave now. Life is short; so don't waste what time you have left being miserable. That is, unless you are willing to have, "A good man for sale."

JUST LISTEN

Trust me, there is a lot you don't know
Trust me, there is a lot I want to tell
At times I am not sure you want to know
Then again I could be wrong
I am scared to be vulnerable
I think you're scared as well
Yes, I don't think the way you do
But that is what makes it interesting
Your moodiness intrigues me
I watch your smile as well as your hips
I love your smell, your touch
I close my eye and I remember your taste
You seem to know my needs
I love that you're eager to learn me

We have something in common
I love your femininity, it is alluring to my eye
If you would just be still
I have more to share
Just listen

TWO

I'm Sure He Knows

Venerability Can Equal Longevity

"Relationship is not a power struggle, yet a union of mind body and spirit." – Drew L. Hinds 2009

I hope you are not a woman who feels that all men cannot be trusted with your heart, so you wear a facade in hopes of protecting yourself. I always believed in the well-known quote by Alfred Lord Tennyson: *"Tis better to have loved and lost than never to have loved at all."* While, I do agree that every man should not have a key to your heart, somewhere along the line you have to take a chance on love and hope for the best. If for any reason it doesn't work, then brush yourself off and try a new relationship with a brand new prospective. The worst thing a woman can do is carry 'mental baggage,' into a new relation. *We all have to let go of our past if we have hopes of pursuing a new relationship of substance.*

SELF-DISCLOSURE

I honestly believe there are many of us (men), who long for a woman to teach us how to love without reserve. Women have always seemed to be in touch with their feelings, and they would be the best suitable teacher in coaching a man in discovering his true feelings. *By opening up to a worthwhile man, a women can take him from existing to living simply by self-disclosing.* When I say a worthwhile man, I am categorizing a man who has understanding and seeks to gain wisdom from a woman who is patient, open minded, and willing to enlighten him. I have also learned that showing vulnerability is really a sign of strength, as oppose to weakness. Though some may beg to differ, think about it for a moment. *It truly takes a strong person to admit that they are wrong, or to reveal their deepest fears with the knowledge that this information could be used against them.* You have to always keep in mind that men are rational creatures, so they need to be taught how to express their feelings. Now, I am not saying that men cannot experience love; I am saying that the expression of it has to be cultivated over a period of time. *I have always thought of love as a verb, an emotion that requires physical effort. Love has to be exercised or it will become stagnant. I don't believe that people fall out of love they just stop exercising it.*

TELL HIM

I have a few questions that I want you to ponder on. Why is it so hard for some women to share their thoughts with men? Why do some men seem to never get beyond a trivial conversation? Why do women stay unsatisfied instead of revealing their frustration? Why do some women feel the need to tell their close friends about their problems instead of the man they are romantically involved with?

Is it just me, or do women have a hard time with self-disclosure; are women aware that men have the same problem? I understand that women have a need to share their intimate thoughts. Ladies, it would help a man to feel validated to hear his woman's thoughts. I am starting to understand that it is a vulnerability issue. Why do women shy away from sharing thoughts with a man? In essence, conversations between men and women seem superficial in nature due to lack of honesty. Men in general have pride and believe that women are aware of this. On the other hand, women feel that it is better not to enlighten him of his inefficiencies, to avoid future resentment. I strongly advise women to tell a man as soon as possible what their grievance are, because a woman will unconsciously gravitate towards someone else to fill that void. Think of confessions as being a proactive measure, as opposed to being reactive and having to apologize for venturing elsewhere.

SENSUALITY

Question: Do you truly believe that sexual compatibility ensures longevity? *I ask this because far too many people use sex as a foundation for a relationship, yet they become confused when it fails the test of time.* Forgive me, but I am amusing myself with the thought of a child getting a new toy. At first, it would seem so gratifying to play without end; yet as time goes on the thrill disappears. Well, let's examine a sexual encounter. In most cases, once two people find a mutual attraction to each other they make a physical advance that may determine if they keep in touch. The problems stem from lack of communication. A sexual encounter means different things between a man and a woman. I have found that women in general have an emotional bond that is initiated prior to a sexual encounter. *To most women, sex means much more than just a sexual void that needs to be filled, and it is usually associated with certain expectations.* Now, this is where communication plays a key. If a woman fails to discuss her expectations prior to a sexual encounter it can lead to utter disaster. *Men, on the other hand, may just want the physical intimacy and nothing more.* At times, a man may assume that a woman understands his intentions due to the fact that he made no mention of anything else other than the sexual act. I have also found that when most women give their bodies to a man, they are expecting it to mean the start of an official committed relationship. It's a shame that most men are not on the same page with the notion of taking her serious after the sexual encounter.

LOVE EXPRESSION

I am starting to believe that we as a society are confused about the topic of physical intimacy. I believe there are more dimensions to physical intimacy then we care to recognize, and this leaves us in a state of false pretense. Let me explain; physical intimacy should be divided into *sensual* and *sexual*.

When I mention *sensual*, I am referring to a love expression that involves a gentle yet reassuring touch. In regards to reassuring touch, it maybe a short massage after a long day, or a firm grip around another's waist while sharing an enduring kiss. Touching your partner in a soothing rhythmic manner, which can set a romantic and submissive state of mind. On the other hand, when I mention *sexual intimacy* I am referring to a person making some form of contact with genitalia. It can cause an immediate mind rushing awareness of self, and leave a person vulnerable.

We must understand that in a committed relationship, having a sense of sexuality is very important, but not a cure. Both parties must constantly engage in sensual encounters to preserve a sense of physical intimacy. Keep in mind that I mentioned sensual as oppose to sexual. *Though sex maybe gratifying in the moment, it lacks the lasting and enduring quality as consistent sensual encounters.* Plus, I have found that a sense of sensuality is less intrusive around both parties' friends or family.

I just had a thought about my own childhood concerning my mother. By talking to my mother, and inquiring about her parents and grandparents, I found that open sensuality was not encouraged in her time. She has always been a hard working Christian woman who believed that cooking and cleaning was her way of expressing her love to her husband. In my later years, I found that my mother had a trying time in expressing her sensuality to her spouse. Mind you, she would spend countless hours telling her friends and colleagues how proud she was. However, she failed to express those same sentiments directly to her immediate partner. I now understand that this was a learned behavior that became a cycle, which was imbedded in females in her family.

People should evaluate themselves and find ways to physically and verbally convey their feelings to those dear to them. The old cliché of they know how I feel really isn't accurate. In fact, relationships may come and go and the person may have no true idea of what they meant to you. Just think of the hurt you could have avoided by just being honest and open about your feelings. I use to hear that, "Love is an action word," and now I believe it. We need to say what we feel to those we love. That is, unless you are willing to have, "A good man for sale."

I WONDER

I wonder what she is thinking when I am late
I wonder what she is thinking when I make excuses
I wonder why she tolerates my impatient nature
I wonder if she noticed I broke her curling iron
I wonder what her and her friends talk about
I wonder if I was just another one of her options
I wonder why she gets quiet when I leave the toilet seat up
I wonder why she never tells me her pain
Sometimes, I wonder how long it will last
Yes, I wonder

THREE

Rewarding Him

Men Need Attention

"Recognition expresses appreciation which is equivalent to a sense of belonging." – Drew L. Hinds 2009

ATTENTION

Men on a whole thrive on positive attention from women. Far too often, verbal reassurance dwindles from a woman once the male publicly announces he is committed. You will be surprised how much a man will go the extra mile to obtain that positive reinforcement from his woman. *I have learned through personal experience that as a man we have emotions and insecurities that only a woman, who is truly tuned to our frequency, can understand.* If a man finds himself far too often begging for attention and mental intimacy from his significant other, he begins to rationalize an alternative partner. In my opinion, men are 75% logical and 25% emotional, which of course is my way of demonstrating a man's balance.

Once a man deciphers that he is receiving the short end of the stick, he will adapt, improvise, and overcome his empty void to acquire his *comfort zone*. I am referring to a man mentally analyzing his situation and finding a rational solution, in some cases a new woman. Most men have no problem finding an alternate route to achieve their happiness. I also mentioned the phrase 'overcome,' which depicts an individual coming to a place of completeness; which in some cases may mean going back to being alone.

Let me ask you a question: should your man have to ask for physical intimacy, and if so why? If your man asks for intimacy, do you think that it's okay to refuse as a form of discipline, and if so why? Ladies please, are you really trying to be alone, why would you consciously turn your man away? Isn't it reasonable to think that your man has a need, and he is coming to you to assist him? Is it true that some women believe that a man can survive without attention (comparing it to a woman restricted from shopping)? Yes, men need to have verbal affirmations, but he should also ensure that his woman is in a positive emotional state to receive his advance. As a woman, be mindful that he will not go too long without physical intimacy. Now, if you both are courting for marriage, then that is a total different story. He maybe more suited to hold out, because he knows that he will be rewarded soon. Ladies, please just keep in mind your man needs attention, so by all means oblige him.

IT'S NOT A REWARD

I have another notion I would like you to take into consideration. Sex is not a reward. Did you catch that? I am serious;

please don't think that you are doing him a favor. *You must come to the realization that physical intimacy is a continuous necessity within a monogamous relationship, not merely a reward.* Trust me on this one; if you continue to think that you can ration out intimacy to your significant other when it's convenient to you, then you are definitely making a sad mistake. Between you, and me men know where to go if they have needs, so please take care of it at home.

Another component of the much-needed attention is communication. Now, anyone who is familiar with my written work understands my strong emphasis on positive communication. You see, communication in my eyes is 80% listening and 20% actual auditory response. Yes, a large portion of communication is *listening*. *When I say listening, I am referring to the art of hearing what is being said, then processing the information and relaying back related elements of the original thought.*

Have you ever had a conversation with someone and felt like they were just not hearing you? Instead it would seem that they are trying to convey their own personal thoughts without listening to yours? *I admit, there are many of us men who tend to ramble on about our self-accomplishments and aspirations; but when you are really into a person, you really don't mind listening attentively.* Chemistry between the both of you should come naturally, as opposed to having to force yourself to stomach a conversation. To be honest, if this is the case, you both may have trouble connecting mentally, and you both need to be honest with each other and go your separate ways.

MAKE HIM SMILE

Whether you want to admit it ladies, you know how to make a man smile (in more ways than one). I have always believed that we should give credit where credit is due. If you have a man that is trying his best to do the right thing, then let him know that you appreciate him. As silly and minuet as it may seem, verbal affirmation goes a long way. I know you know some sentimental attributes that stimulate your man, take some time out and surprise him. Whether you have a man that is into sports or is an intellectual, you should get to know him so you can reward him accordingly. Many times we take the little things for granted and overlook the obvious - please don't fall into that realm of complacency.

Always find time to let your man know how much you appreciate him, you will be surprised to know that many times they haven't the faintest idea. Men for the most part are not mind readers and they don't strive to be either. *You have to make things black and white for a man, simply say what you mean and mean what you say.* Don't ever think that a man doesn't know what he wants due to the fact that he doesn't demand it. Some men are different and passive in nature, and they may have to be asked before they divulge their needs.

GET IT TOGETHER

As it relates to affection, a man is like a baby: he would rather be breast fed than given a bottle. Everyone should be in tuned with his or her sexuality, and they should know how to physically cater to a man without using alternative means. Ok, I see that lost look on your face. No man should have to go to an adult entertainment center when he has a woman in his life, nor should he have to admire other women online when his woman is a phone call away. What's wrong with this picture? Well, whether you want to face the facts or not, you may not be connecting with him physically. Men are visual creatures, and they tend to touch in order to verify what they see. *Don't panic ladies: if you enticed him in the initial part of the relationship, then you can do it again at will.* Find out what your man likes about you physically and you have partially won the battle. Next, learn how to use those physical attributes to your advantage. I personally like to depict physical intimacy as two parts: sensual and sexual. Combined, sensual and sexual intimacy provides a sense of sensuality. Once you have mastered the art of your sensuality, then you can rest assured knowing that he can't wait to receive your rewards.

I truly believe that everyone has an innate need to feel needed and appreciated, regardless of gender or status. *I also believe that attention shouldn't come from sheer obligation, but a real emotional tie.* Remember, having someone in your life is not a right, but a privilege. Women, I urge you to be honest with your significant other and tell them your expectations. By revealing your true needs, then you will open an avenue for him to open up and disclose his need for attention. That is, unless you are willing to have, "A good man for sale."

MY REWARD

I still can't believe that you are mine
You give me such joy as you beckon my intimacy
Your lips stay sweet, as if to summon my masculinity
I long for your kiss, which is light yet fulfilling

You have given life to a hopeless man
I yearn for your seductive embrace
Your body caters to my longing
I am at ease in your bosom
I forget my woes inside your love
I am blessed to have you
My love
My friend
My reward

FOUR

Knowing Your Role

Knowing Why He Choose You

"One should reveal their true expectations in the conception of a union to avoid misconceptions and future strife."
– Drew L. Hinds 2009

It may seem funny, but I have grown to understand that there are women who have no clue as to why their man chose them; which explains why some women fail to understand how to keep him. You see we all have expectations that need to be fulfilled. Men gravitate towards supportive women who are strong in nature, yet *meek in character.* I am referring to a woman who can see potential and is willing to help empower a man's true potential. Men as a whole need women who are not afraid to admit their flaws, and who are willing to receive love in its uncultivated form. When our expectations are not met, then we (for lack of better words), "Spoil our appetite." Only by having a good means of communication (80% listening and 20% verbalization), can we achieve the goal of knowing why our significant other has chosen us in their life. There was a woman from my past who told me that my concerns were petty.

Well, maybe to her that may have been the case, but it made all the difference to me and caused me to withdraw. One has to understand that if a concern has any relevance to the opposing party, then one should understand that attacking another's character is simply destructive.

HIS EYES

Let's start with the basics. Do you know what goes through a man's mind at first glance? Well let me help clarify so there will be no further misunderstanding. *When a man sees a shapely woman (with hips and assets included), he basically thinks that she is sexy based on her physical attributes, point blank.* Of course, all other senses stop functioning for a brief moment because he is instinctively visually stimulated. Don't panic ladies, just hope that it's you that is causing the visual stimulus. It's funny, even if a woman isn't the most attractive in her facial features, a man will be attracted to a woman's body alone, making her automatically sexy. *On the other hand, if a woman has a beautiful face, but lacks a well-toned body, then a man usually categorizes her as pretty.* Men usually don't chase after a pretty woman for long if she doesn't seem to have any other attributes to keep him interested. To be honest, I have known men who are attracted to women with a sexy shape, yet they lack an appealing face. In this case, a man will secretly become intimate with her, but he won't let anyone know that they're an item or see them together in public. I see your expression: I guess it's just a guy thing. *Oh, I almost forgot, in the case where you have a woman who has both a beautiful face and a flawless body, then and only then is she considered, "Fine."* You would be surprised to know though, that a man will chase a sexy body, with a nice face (a fine woman), until he runs out of money, gas, or Viagra.

Okay, brief overview ladies: work on a becoming a woman of substance. *The superficial aspect is alluring to the eye, but lacks substance and the guarantee of longevity.* It is definitely a plus, in this day and age, to cultivate a spiritual awareness as well as a new mental consciousness. One more thing ladies, and brace yourselves for this one. I am going to try to be politically correct, if that is possible… (sigh). Now, please understand that there are many women who know how to carry themselves in a manner that truly accentuates their shape; but there are those women who really need to ask for assistance and use better discretion. I am very happy to see women who are plus sized regain a sense of self worth in our modern society, and I applaud them. On the other hand, I personally believe that it should not be the end result. Be happy with who you are, but always strive for better (in all aspects of life) - one should not be stagnant. Be honest with yourself, obesity is the number one leading cause of diabetes, cardio, and respiratory illnesses.

Always keep in mind ladies, that men are visually stimulated, at all times, no matter what age, financial status, race, and religion. So, even though you both have kids together and your body has changed, due to age and circumstances, he is still visually stimulated the same as always. *A woman should never rationalize that it is all right to just let themselves go, or fall into a false pretense that their man is fine with her giving up on her appearance.* Another food for thought I would like to share is that men like to be able to physically carry their woman. Let's compare it to a mother and her child: when the child cries, or has done well in a task, the mother picks up the child and embraces them. With that said, there really isn't a difference in how a man enjoys lifting and embracing his woman (call it a psychological thing). Let me elaborate just a little more. A man enjoys being able to lift up his woman in his arms, which in most cases leads to sensual intimacy. Psychologically, it makes him feel that he can protect her and care for her (hence the tradition of carrying her across the threshold).

You do know that most committed men won't say anything about your physical features changing, but I promise you, he is thinking it. To avoid sleeping on the coach he will mask his concern that is unless you pressure him and he verbalizes out of frustration. Please note that I am by no means vindicating this behavior, just explaining it. I found that there are men who feel the need to make a woman feel guilty about their obese size and appearance. As a result, these men resort to verbally taunting women by calling them derogatory names. This behavior is not constructive, and no woman should ever tolerate this negative behavior: it is a form of verbal abuse. Take into consideration that this particular man has subconsciously lost the visual stimulus, and in his mind he is verbally giving the woman notice. At this stage it is still not too late for both parties to correct the concern, but it will take a joint effort. The male in this case will have to learn to be patient and encouraging, and the female counterpart will have to regain self-pride and physically change her mental and physical disposition.

SUPPORT SYSTEM

Every man needs a support system, regardless of his status. You see, a man can only go but so far without a woman; but he needs a woman to help maintain his momentum. I do apologize for all men who have failed to be honest in conveying their need for a resourceful woman who can help him when he is overwhelmed. I want you to understand that there is a difference between hope and direction. I am depicting the belief that something positive will occur in time through patience and diligence. In my eyes, direction is a path that one takes for their own life, which correlates to who they are and what they strive to accomplish. I have noticed that there are some women who are under the false pretense that they were put on earth to give men direction; I for one don't agree, and believe me, I am not alone. I do, however agree that a woman can help a man find his true potential, but it is up to a man to decipher who he is and where he is going with his life.

TRUE WORTH

Believe me when I say, "Only a woman of sound character can keep a man of worth." Yes, I did say, "A man of worth." *You see, all men are not worth keeping.* Do yourself a favor and leave any person who makes you feel less of a woman, or doesn't appreciate what you have to offer. Far too many times I have come across women who have low self-esteem, and then they began acting out of character. I am speaking about a person who is frustrated with their present circumstance and begins arguments or engages in activities to get attention. For example, having an affair. In one isolated scenario, a woman stated that cheating gave her a sense of power over her man. Now you and I both know that this behavior solves nothing; it is a cry for help. This scenario also brings us back to positive communication, where both parties should feel free to share their deepest concerns. A man won't commit himself to a woman unless he believes that she is trust worthy, has maturity, and can help bring balance to his life. I am using the word balance in retrospect to a man finding a woman to help him find his true potential.

I mentioned maturity, meaning to be conscious of another's needs. I have also found that maturity is needed in order to enable one to cater to someone else's needs above them self. *You see, you get what you give, and in a relationship one should give without regard for receiving.* In essence, a relationship is a selfless act. I have finally grasped the notion that only a mature woman can take the time to familiarize herself with her man, and adapt to his world. Be mindful that I was careful not to say, "Change who she is or what she stands for," yet simply learn him (both in and out). *It can be catastrophic when a woman attempts to recreate a man's world in hopes of accommodating herself.* Trust me, a man may not discover a woman's ulterior motives to revamp his vision of life at first, but when he does it won't end well. I have yet to meet a man who enjoys being manipulated. That is, unless you are willing to have "A good man for sale."

NAGGING

Yes, I have to discuss this, for the simple fact that many of you wonderful women have entered into the realm of nagging a man… (sigh). Yes, I understand that the majority of the time, the point you're trying to convey is relevant to the situation, but let's be honest, the manner in which you relay your message can be counter productive. Let's back up, you are trying to convey to your man that his car doesn't have enough gas to get to his desired destination, and he seems to be ignoring your concern. So, you take it upon yourself to repeat your concern every five seconds until he finally pulls into a gas station.

In another case, you both may be planning on entertaining guests at your place, and you would like him to get freshened up, so you remind him every time you make eye contact with his silhouette. Now, in both cases you truly feel that you are assisting him in his endeavors and yes, you do mean well; but do you really know what he is thinking? First of all, you have to understand that this is not the first time your man's vehicle has been low on fuel and men are logical and usually have a system. I know you are wearing that look like "whatever;" that must be the same system that got us lost with no gas last time.

I know it sounds weird, but you have to allow a man to figure things out all his own. Think of it like this: when you have kids it seems like you are always trying to save them from making careless mistakes, and as time goes on you realize that as much as you warn them they still feel the need to make their own mistakes. So, with that said, think of a man as a big kid that needs to make his own mistakes, in order to learn from it. *It's better for a man to make a mistake and face it, than you repeatedly instructing him every step of the way*. That is, unless you don't mind having "A good man for sale."

JUST FOR ME

I choose you for you, I love your eyes
I choose you to calm my spirit, I love your shapely curves
I choose you to inspire my vision, I love your warm embrace
I choose you to bring me back to reality, I love your soft kiss
I choose you to love me in and out of season, I love your honesty

I choose you to bare my child, I love your mental intimacy
I choose you to pray for me, I love your seductive gaze
I choose you for so many reasons, but mostly it was just for me

FIVE

Choosing Happiness

Men Know When They Are Unhappy

"Men think black and white simply because they are rational creatures, so they will express their discomfort. The trick is to listen and empathize, regardless of your own perspective." – Drew L. Hinds 2009

GOSSIP

I was speaking to a female friend of mine and she expressed that she noticed that men really don't take reprimanding well. She began reflecting on personal instances where she noticed how men shut down and somewhat internalize their discomfort. She went on to share that she had found a scripture that shed some light on the conversation. *"Better to dwell in a corner of a housetop, than in a house shared with a contentious woman," Proverbs 21:9 NKJV.* I of course laughed at the notion, you see it really amazes me that most women seem to have to go through trial and error to recognize the age old fact: "Men can't stand a Nagging Woman." Half way through the conversation she began reprimanding her man due to what she had heard about him. At that moment I had to stop her.

Ladies, if there is anything that can destroy a happy home, its gossip. I define gossip as information that is exchanged between people, who wish nothing more than to spread negativity, and in some cases, lies. I have noticed, that some people put down others in hopes of making themselves feel better. There is a saying that comes from the play Doctor Faustus written by Christopher Marlowe; found in Scene 5 Line 42 *"Solamen miseris socios habuisse doloris."* Which translates as, "Misery loves company". Please, don't let gossip be the reason you loose a good man. Take into consideration that most of the information shared is false, and are created to discredit someone fueled by jealousy.

GOOD

I can see that look on your face; do I have to learn all of this to get and keep his attention? Well, to be honest the trick is… to just be you. You see, you don't want a man to be attracted to you under false pretenses. In other words, if you don't normally dress provocatively because you really are a conservative person, then don't. The worst thing you could do is force yourself to be someone you are not just to get his attention. A man really doesn't appreciate when he falls for a, 'fairytale woman.' This is a woman who uses deceit to attract men for her own ulterior motives. A man admires a woman who is confident in who she is and what she stands for; yet humble enough to accept criticism or compliments.

Men are attracted to women who are aware of their sexuality and can attract positive attention. This type of woman can be attractive without coming across as provocative or conceited. A man likes a woman who can run things at the office, yet knows how to submit to a level headed man at home without an argument. A man needs a supportive woman that can appreciate his positive traits, yet persuasively compels him to rise above his negatives. If a man knows that he can trust you, and that you have his best interest in mind, then he will slowly open up to you in time. Men are stubborn by nature, and they need a patient woman who is willing to teach them the importance of mental intimacy. I use my mental intimacy concept to signify the act of individuals that can stimulate each other emotionally, simply through engaging in captivating conversation. It truly is an art, because I have noticed that not everyone possesses this skill. Achieving mental intimacy allows the opposing party listening to feel calm, yet intrigued. It also arouses a yearning for more conversation, which equates into quality time. Trust me, if a woman can make a man laugh at will, then it usually is a key indication that she has achieved some form of mental intimacy and the ball is definitely in her corner.

BAD

Now let me enlighten you on what really repels a man. In a prudent man's mind, sight and touch are usually the main senses that are used in stimulation. Hearing of course goes hand in hand with the mental intimacy concept we previously discussed, but these same senses that can stimulate a man can also do the opposite. I have spoken with quite a few men who are puzzled with women who aren't consistent. If you met your man when you were athletic and out going, it would behoove you to maintain that image. You see, this is one of that attributes that attracted him. I understand that we outgrow activities, but be mindful the effect it may have on your existing relationship.

The next big item I am going to attempt to tackle is insecurity. I have come to understand that there are many types of signs of insecurity, but I am going to only discuss a few that can really take a toll on a meaningful relationship. There are many people who suffer from mental baggage, which if not treated, can evolve into insecurity. A woman may be experiencing insecurities when she finds herself: going through his cell phone, following him around town, calling around to track him down, having him taking a blood test every other month, becoming jealous of any female associates he may have, fearing that he may leave due his new success, and interrogating her man as to his phone conversations. It is definitely time for a good man to just pack his bags and leave when he has: been honest about his whereabouts, introduce her to his friends, discontinued contact with old flames, and she is still blaming him for her insecurities.

I have also found that there are women who have insecurities that attempt to fill their voids with material gain: such as expensive clothes, hair, and jewelry. If a woman superimposes her shopping obsession on a man, it can cause a financial hardship and a visible rift between the couple. Far too many times when a woman has been raised with the notion that she should get everything she wants, the relationships end in disaster. Yes, there are men that will try to accommodate this complex (as a means to an ends), but far too often it ends sooner than later. The problem stems when a woman's wants become costly to a man's patience and income. You would be surprised how many women really believe that expensive gifts determine whether or not a man is worthy of their companionship.

In reality, the obsessive need for monetary and tangible gifts reveal the obvious shallowness of a woman. *So, to all my high maintenance women, enjoy your possessions, because they may be your only comfort on a lonely night.*

INDIFFERENT

Ok, why are you giving me that look again? It would behoove you to come to the understanding that if you are displaying any of these attributes, you really don't need to be in any form of relationship just yet. In fact, it wouldn't hurt to attempt to find some sort of spiritual peace, or maybe a good therapist to clarify things. In this state of mind, you can do nothing positive to help improve the present relationship. *A person needs time alone to learn to love them self and learn accountability for their own actions.* Another thought that I wouldn't want you to overlook is cause and effect. If you do something negative, then be mindful of a possible undesirable outcome. Have you noticed that people who don't take accountability for their actions usually find themselves playing the victim role? These people are under the impression that the world is against them, instead of taking responsibility for their life. It is essential that they make a conscious decision to stop playing the victim role, because in most cases they are the cause of their issues. I find it hard to believe that these individuals don't have anyone in their lives that can point out their character flaws; more often these individuals are in denial. Unconsciously, this person can give off a negative vibe, and create a negative environment within the relationship. Taking responsibility for ones action is a sign of maturity, and can lead to a better you. Oh, its true, finding a good man is a rare commodity, so be nice, you may not have a second chance.

JEALOUSY

Yes, it is that serious that it needs its own title. I want you to understand that jealousy may seem minuet in comparison to other relationship issues, but bear in mind that it is usually the foundation of many issues as well. I mentioned gossip earlier in this chapter, and in my opinion, it stems from a *jealous nature*. I am referring to someone who wants to have more than another person has, due to their own insecurities. Once a person takes on a mindset of jealousy, it becomes hard for that individual to rationalize, effectively communicate, trust, or receive love.

I want you to first understand that jealousy is a learned behavior, and so it can be unlearned with a *conscious effort*. I am referring to a person first acknowledging their disposition. Secondly, they must find innovative ways to dispel their jealousy that is constructive. Finally, there must be self-disclosure between both partners in the relationship, explaining the origin of the jealousy. A supportive man will consciously make an effort to reassure his lady that she can trust him with her intimate feelings.

One must learn to give those they care about the benefit of the doubt; in doing so, it helps to eliminate the elements that feed into jealousy. Next, find out what you are truly jealous about and why. Could it be mental baggage from your past? Try to write out your concerns and then review them at a later date when you have had time to cool off. Sometimes it is best to review issues when you have had ample time to assess the overall situation. Find a mentor who can give you unbiased advice concerning your jealous temperament. Many times, jealousy stems from insecurities that we have internalized. For example, you may be jealous of someone with long hair because you have been unable to grow yours to a desired length. One must try being honest about their personal insecurities before they can overcome jealousy.

RELAX

I am with you by choice not by court order, so relax
I paid the parking meter and as well as your mom's bill, so relax
I love you regardless of your new size, so relax
I am sorry you had a rough day at work, but its Friday, so relax
I am sorry the recipe came out wrong, we can eat out, so relax
I know you can only work part time as a student
That's why I work, so relax
You can't have any more kids, well neither can I afford it, so relax
No really, relax

SIX

Be Honest

Men Need To Know If You Are Both On The Same Page

"Why initiate a relationship on false pretense, it has no substance or longevity?" – Drew L. Hinds 2009

BROKEN WOMEN

I was speaking to an old friend of mine who expressed that she has a habit of testing men when she becomes involved. She went on to explain that instead of expressing how she felt to the guy, she would start arguments and attempt to provoke the man to see if he would get angry and ultimately leave. She felt that this was the only way to see if a man loved her unconditionally. Well, the truth is that this behavior is very destructive, and it is like playing Russian Roulette. If she continues this behavior, then one of two outcomes could occur. The male could get frustrated and leave, or it could even end in a physical altercation depending on the type of man and his background. Ladies, just be honest with a man and tell him what you need and ask him were he is in his life. It is all a gamble, but if you are not honest from the beginning, then there is no one else to blame.

There are many broken women who have been hurt in the past, so they resort to unorthodox methods to find true love. Ladies, you must let go of mental baggage that you may be carrying. *If you truly want to love again you must release the pain you have by forgiving those who have physically and emotionally abused you.* You must understand that forgivingness is more so for your benefit then those you are forgiving. These negative thoughts can cause stress, which results in physical and mental illnesses. It has been said that if a patient man can find it in his heart to love a broken woman in spite of her emotional conditions; then she will cherish him for life. Ladies, don't lose hope, there is a man alive that will cater to you; the trick is to distinguish him from all the imposters. Trust me, when a man loves a woman, she knows. The problem is that so many women fall for men that they know are bad for their health. *First, if a man doesn't fit your moral standards, then don't even waist your time investing in him.* Yes, relationship is an investment. *So, for all you women spending years in a dead end relationship and have nothing to show for it, you have made a bad investment.* Please, just be honest with yourselves ladies. You know what you deserve in comparison to what you are tolerating. Don't you believe you deserve your own man; one you don't have to share with some other unknown woman? *For once in your life, take control of your emotions and make a rational decision to mutually love someone who loves you back.*

THE PAST

Prior to me contemplating marriage, I ran into someone from

my past. At first I was a bit apprehensive, but I remained polite. My mind wandered on how I always had mixed feelings for this person. I always admired how she concerned herself with my well being, and how she never lacked affection. I reminisced about the long peaceful evenings cuddling and sharing ideas and dreams. Then I was reminded of the reckless and childish behavior that pushed me away. It's funny though, seeing her now after all those years with what appears to be a new level of maturity and decorum. I was intrigued.

We agreed to keep in contact. Over a short period of time, I vigilantly studied my newly found significant other, although she was from my past. Her demeanor was different, her poses, and gestures new. Her renewed gracefulness was alluring to my eye and I was captivated, yet cautious. Yes, a lot had changed over the course of time. I decided to finally let my guard down and embrace the present, only to find something totally out of place.

She had become career driven, and had no time for quiet evenings with insightful conversations. She had lost her zeal to comfort and nurture a man's spirit. She was independent and self-sufficient, no longer waiting for my endorsement of her endeavors. Yes, I was proud of her, but in all of the modifications and pronounced growth, she had changed the essence of whom I fell in love with. She had grown in stature, but not spirit. She had matured financially, but not in character. She had mastered the art of persuasion, but not forgiveness. She had overcome insecurities, but not mental baggage. She had gained a new respect from her peers, but not from my heart. I now know that all the little things I fell in love with had been outgrown, and with that growth, I had no choice but to leave my past love alone.

UNEQUALLY YOKED

Have you ever stopped to notice that there are many of us who choose our mates with our eyes? Sometimes it's because of peer pressure, and we end up with a relationship that the bible describes as being "*unequally yoked.*" What it is *Unequally Yoked?* This is a concept that has long been understood as both parties in a relationship being of different religious beliefs; but that is only one aspect of it. To be "*unequally yoked*," or simply a poor match, also refers to a couple that does not have the same mindset or the same outlook on life. These differences can be based on how to raise children, or deciding whether or not the wife will be a stay-at-home mom as opposed to working mom. Many couples really don't communicate well enough, and they don't come to the realization that they are really not on the same page.

I am starting to realize that we have the concept all wrong. We should not work hard to maintain a relationship because of our selfish endeavors. We must not allow our egos or outside forces destroy our relationship. A relationship should be comfortable: it should flow with ease. Neither party should walk on thin ice to maintain the relationship. *I am under the impression that some people are so scared of being alone that they force themselves to bear all types of hardships*. Is it really worth the aggravation and stress just to have companionship? Why do we settle? Surely, we can all do badly by ourselves, yet we stay in the relationship from hell and do worse. It reminds me of a story I heard as a child about Samson and Delilah, *(Judges 16: 1-31)*. In this story, Samson had a weakness for prostitutes and he tried to turn one into a housewife, which ultimately caused his death.

So many of us never wait to know who it is we are marrying, yet it will be revealed in due time. Instead, we rush into a situation, have children, accumulate bills together and waste many years being unhappy and feeling alone. *Now, if we could only grasp the concept that we cannot control our circumstance. We can control how we react to circumstances and as a result we would have a better disposition in life*. Too many times we claim to stay in a relationship for the children, and then we justify why we have affairs outside of our marriages, thereby spoiling our appetite.

LET IT BE KNOWN

If I may be so bold, let me make it clear that no man desires a lazy woman in any aspect, race, color, religion, shape or size. Okay, why do you have that bewildered look on your face? I am serious; men in general do not appreciate a lazy woman. You may or may not have heard of the term "virtuous woman," which is equivalent to a diligent woman. *You see no matter your background, you should never allow your man to entertain the notion that you are indeed a lazy woman.* A good man can see potential, and he is usually willing and capable of supporting a woman's growth. He also possesses patience to work alongside a woman who has a teachable spirit.

Men on a whole, desire to have a woman that can be supportive emotionally and financially. A lazy woman truly has no use to a man or to herself for that matter. If you would, explain to me what benefit would a woman have to a man if she has no ambition or self motivation to better herself, other than becoming a burden? *There are many of us men who desire to have what is known as a 'power couple,' where both parties bring their talents and resources to the table to become more successful socially and financially.* If a woman is mindful of being diligent in helping her man succeed she will be openly appreciated. On the other hand if a woman solely relies on her good looks she will remain a mere trophy. *Keep in mind that trophies are known to be collected, so you won't be the only one on his shelf.*

CAUSE & EFFECT

Well, I believe I can safely say that we all understand that most of us attempt to put our best foot forward when we initially meet a person of interest (and that is fine). I believe the problems arise when either party fails to reveal that they have some real deep dark secrets. The kind of secrets that would cause the average person to turn around and run as fast as their legs can carry them. So, what do most do? They hide their secrets in fear of being rejected. Can you see where we are definitely started off on a bad foot?

In Mark 4:22 NKJV it says, *"For there is nothing hidden which will not be revealed, nor has anything been kept secret but that it should come to light."* Let me ask you a question: can you imagine the repercussions when one person you care about finds out about your deceit? Mind you, if you really have given up on saving your relationship, then that is another story; but those who care should take action to rectify. Oh, so you want an example? Let's just say you have three kids, you just got out of jail, you have a $30,000 judgment on your credit, and you can't find your husband to get a legal divorce. Well, I think that a decent guy might want to know about your skeleton bones, especially when he engages in any form of intimacy with you. It is always nice too know that you are still married in the preliminary conversations. Ladies, you would be surprised that the truth would really set you free. Why, you ask? *Well, let's just say that there are men that will accept you just the way you are; they just don't appreciate any surprises* (especially if it's a sex change).

I just had a thought, which was in conjunction with our earlier discussion concerning honesty. Trust me, I am aware of women who have tried to trick unsuspecting men into bed to purposely get pregnant. In some cases women believe that this will guarantee that they will acquire their green card. I have also come across women who are married, and because they are upset with their spouse, they want to become intimate with someone else to get back at their man. I have witnessed women who have stepped outside their relationship due to the fact that their man is away in the military, college, a business trip, or hospitalized. I am telling you, men have had many different instances where women have had ulterior motives. The end result of women deceiving men is usually decent men turning into dishonest men (as self-defense). These men vow never again to trust another pretty face due to being emotionally devastated by a failed relationship.

Question: If you know that your man wants to have kids of his own, shouldn't you let him know that you have no intention of having any? It may be a medical issue that hinders you from baring children; does he have the right to know? Time and time again, I have heard of couples that have faced such problems. They usually end in resentment and separations. I believe it is selfish to withhold information from your spouse due to the fear of losing him. Be honest, you wouldn't want someone to mislead you into a situation without your consent?

I have also come to the conclusion that some women have a hard time being honest with men, simply because they don't know their true feelings. For instance, a woman breaks up with her recent boyfriend and six months later she meets a nice guy. It so happens that this nice guy wants to settle down with her, but there is a problem. It would seem that the lady in his life doesn't really know how she truly feels about her present significant other because she still has mixed emotions for her old boyfriend. So, instead of being upfront she decided to string her present man along to fill the void for companionship. But at the same time, she is avoiding the fact that he needs to know where he stands in her life. Well, how can she be honest when she really isn't sure herself? The problem some individuals fail to understand is that you don't have to have all the answers, but it is always best to allow yourself to be *transparent*. I am referring to just letting the person who you are involved with know the truth to your situation. Allow your man to make a conscious decision on his own concerning staying involved. In this situation, being dishonest is the worst thing she could do. In the end, he will have no choose but to rely on false pretense. That is, unless she is willing to have, "A good man for sale."

QUESTION

Please be honest with me, I am curious
Where do you go after we argue?
Is that really your hair, if not how much was it?
Do you really think your mom hates me?
Why does your male boss always call you after hours?
Have you dated some of your male friends?
Is it me or do you hate when I go to the gym alone?
Why do you always ask for money when you get paid?
If you're my woman, why do you always seem too busy for me?
Why do you always leave the gas tank empty?
When it's your time of the month, can I work late?
To be honest, I am happy, I was just curious

SEVEN

Security Check

Emotional vs. Tangible

"Women need emotional security, but men need a tangible source of physical connection to achieve the equivalent of her emotion."
– Drew L. Hinds 2009

GENDER SECURITY

Face it, we all have needs, and the better we understand each other needs the easier it will be to maintain a meaningful relationship. There seems to be some misunderstanding between men and women on the subject of security. *Most men understand security (in a relationship), to mean financially secure, among other possessions.* On the other hand, I have found that women see it a little differently. *Security for a woman stems from an emotional standpoint that she is loved and can trust her man with her intimate thoughts and fears.* I hear women explain to their spouse that they need security, and the man just sits there with a blank stare, because he is making six figures a year.

This concept is what I refer to as, "*Gender Security.*" You see, security means two different things for men and women. Society has molded men into the mindset that they are the provider, the breadwinner, and the protector. *So as men, there is a gravitation towards believing that with financial stability comes the equivalence of happiness.* Now you tell me: if you have money, are you truly happy with money alone? Money by itself does not equate to happiness: it just makes life easier. Money should only be a commodity, not a necessity when it relates to a relationship. *As for the ladies, security is simply an emotional venture.* You see women need to know that they are more important than any superficial possession money can buy! You see, men know that a real woman will love him for him, not what he owns. A man should humble himself and allow a woman to teach me how to love her from the inside out, which would bring about an emotional security.

Ladies, please do yourself a favor and don't antagonize a man when you don't feel the presence of the emotional security you require. Take action to show him what emotional security feels like. For example, give your man a call and ask him if you can drop off something at his job. Then prepare a lunch for him, get dressed, look your best, deliver in person, and compliment him on his appearance. You could even send him flowers at work with a secret admirer note that has a nickname that only both of you know. These thoughtful acts can be done every so often to express your appreciation, and in return he will feel compelled to return the sentiment.

WHO MAKES THE MONEY?

Tell me, do I really need to express how finances can depress a man? Are you not aware that a man can feel emasculated, due to the fact that his woman makes more money than him? Have you ever thought about the effect that a man losing his job has, causing him to depend on his woman for financial support? If you find yourself in a situation where your man has had some financial setback, please tread softly. A man can self-destruct depending on how strong his will is during such a trying time. Most men don't operate well when they feel helpless; so don't antagonize him when he is down and out. *A man will react one of two ways when confronted about their issues, either they will shut down or lash out.* It might be better to get his close friends to encourage him through his trying times. Let him know that you have appreciated what he has done so far, and allow him to still make decision within the relationship. By allowing the man to continue in his position of leadership regardless of his financial crisis, allows him still save face, and it will make the transition easier.

Another concept I developed that I would like to share with you is, the *'Male Ego Factor.'* This suggests that a man has the ability to lead, provide, and protect his family. If there is any opposing force that challenges the male's sanctum, then the *'Male Ego Factor,'* automatically initiates to preserve his self-worth. I have realized this to be more so a learned behavior. I say this due to the fact that all men do not possess this characteristic. Men who have been exposed to an influential male role model tend to gravitate towards the "*Male Ego Factor*."

It would seem that most men are perceived as strong and emotionless, or incapable of feeling worthlessness; however, this is not true. Men, like women, can feel worthless, but they display it far differently than women. For this reason, men's feelings are often overlooked, and this causes a man to feel inclined to defend his pride or, *"Male Ego Factor."* Now that we have a better understanding of this concept, let me add one more thought. It would be wise not to corner a man you care for into a state-of-mind where he feels like he is being stripped of his masculinity. In essence, ignoring a man's *"Male Ego Factor"* can affect the overall atmosphere of the family setting.

FORGIVENESS

As we all know, divorce rates are at an all time high, and I believe that it is mainly due to one of three things: *communication, honesty,* and *forgiveness.* I am going to solely focus on forgiveness in this section. I want you to keep in mind that couples don't separate simply because they are a bad match. *The problems that exist are due to the fact that both individuals lack the knowledge and patience to deal with each other.* Patience is intertwined with forgiveness, and it can really make all the difference. The Word says, "*And be ye kind one to another, tenderhearted, forgiving one another, even as God for Christ sake hath forgiven you,*" Ephesians 4:32 (KJV).

Believe me when I say that forgiveness is not an easy task, yet vital to the healing phase. A great approach to forgiveness is accepting that we are all human and imperfect, as the Word says, "For all have sinned, and come short of the glory of God;" (Romans 3:23, KJV). Now, I do not want you for any reason to think that negative behavior should be condoned (such as the cheating and secrecy that was conveyed in the story). In fact, one should set a personal standard of living, which exemplifies their expectations for others in the family. *However, we should not impose our standards of living on others and expect them to behave as we do.*

I was speaking to a friend, and she began to tell me of a sermon that she heard. The speaker stated, "We should be childlike, not childish." He went on to explain that children naturally say what is on their mind, share their feelings openly, and instinctively let them go. Reflect with me awhile—a child is playing on the playground and another kid steps on their new shoes. Immediately they respond: "You stepped on my new shoes. That was mean; and I am not your friend anymore." Nonetheless, by the next recess, both children are friends again. As kids, we had the right concept: we expressed our true feelings, accepted feedback, and we let go of the hurt. We truly see the application of Matthew 18:21,22 (KJV), which states: *"Then came Peter to him, and said, Lord, how often shall my brother sin against me, and I forgive him? Till seven times? Jesus saith unto him, I say not unto thee, until seven times: but until seventy times seven."*

I really want you to understand that forgiveness is not meant only to pardon the opposing party. It is also the key in releasing your pain as you begin your mental and emotional cleansing. *Ultimately, I see relationships (of all types) as an investment, and if someone that you have invested in betrays your trust, you must first forgive and heal in order to restore your balance.* Once your balance has been restored, and you are able to look at the situation objectively, then you must decide whether or not it is a sound investment to keep certain individuals in your time and space. As I have said, *"It is a privilege for someone to be in your life, not a right."*

WILL HE STAY

I often hear women ask, *"Why do I feel that he is going to leave me?"* Well, to be honest, if you have reached to the point in your relationship where you have reason to believe that your man is displeased with the relationship as a whole, then you probably are right. You definitely need to seek immediate damage control to mend the damaged relationship. You may want to also consider that men need *emotional security* as well. Don't laugh I am serious. Now when I say *emotional security* as it relates to men, I am referring to knowing how to cater to a man's needs. I think it is safe to say that men are visually and physically stimulated, but if you can find a way to ease his mind from the stresses of his day, then you are closer to soothing him emotionally.

I have noticed at times that women can be self-observed, and they overlook the fact that men need to be pampered. Let me give you the honest truth: a man needs to receive intimacy to help him relax. Why do you look so confused, you do understand that it's the truth, right? When I say *intimacy*, please understand that I am referring to both physical and mental. Most men seem to be introverts and keep all of their problems to themselves. *Encourage a man to relax by stimulating his sight and touch, then persuade him to release his thoughts too you.* Try not to interrupt him, just allow him to unload all the concerns on his mind. Now if he asks for your opinion then be cautious and ask him how it makes him feel. *Don't try to solve his problems, just let him share without being judged.*

A man requires his *physical needs* fulfilled as well. Yes, I am referring to his sexual needs. In fact, a man will put up with your nagging if he knows at the end of the day you will make it up to him, in more ways than one. *A healthy sex life is vital to a healthy monogamous relationship.* Try to be very open with your man concerning your sexuality. Find out what pleases your spouse and also share what you desire. Quite naturally, if you cater to him, he will be more inclined to cater to you… (hint, hint). *You would be surprised how physical intimacy helps your man release his stress; in fact he would look forward to coming home to get your therapy.* Always cater to your man's needs before you reveal your personal issues. Trust me on this one, if you help him, then he will naturally feel compelled to serve you. That is, unless you are willing to have, "A good man for sale."

I'M YOUR MAN

Yes, I am with you for more reasons than one
Trust me, it's not for your finances, you're broke
I love when you don't question me
Then again, I planned on telling you anyway
You're beautiful, even though you lost your shape
I know you gained since we first met, so what
I like that you know me and can make me smile
You seem to know when to stop me before I lose it
Then again you know how to get me started
I can't stand you at times, but I am helpless alone
So, yes I am your man, what else is new

EIGHT

Do You Know Him?

Knowing of Him vs. Knowing Him

"Knowing someone from the inside out goes deeper than a superficial observation; yet it is a true mental intimacy that transcends time and space." – Drew L. Hinds 2009

LET'S DANCE

I had a thought I wanted to share with you ladies. Have you ever considered that every man you are attracted to isn't guaranteed to be the right one for you? In other words, what you want isn't always what you need. I believe that we all at some point get caught up with the superficial aspects of dating, such as: looks, and status that we loose ourselves in all the hype. *It really takes a sound-minded person to evaluate a new prospective partner with logic, prior to allowing emotions to validate the choice.*

Think of relationship like a dance. First, a man approaches and asks you for a dance. At this point you have a choice to accept or decline: remember that it is a privilege as opposed to a right to dance with you. Once you have accepted his offer you observe his movements - his technique. A lot can be deciphered by observation: is he experienced, can he make decisions under pressure, is he sensitive to your needs and is he willing to compromise? You can also see if he is truly into you or easily distracted by all the other females lustfully staring at him. Before a dance ends, you always know what you have experienced, and how it felt. I think that the problem exists when you are not being honest with yourself, and not accepting the fact that this man is not a suitable dance partner. Many of us are so scared of dancing alone that we settle for a bad experience on the dance floor of life.

So, the next time a man approaches you, be prepared to accept the dance of a lifetime. If by any chance you are pleased, then by all means vocalize your pleasure before he decides to dance with someone else. Tell him that you adore the way he gracefully, yet firmly, holds the small of your back as he glides you across the floor. Praise him for patiently allowing you to adjust to his masculine frame as he lifts you from the dance floor. Enlighten him of his charming smile and of his alluring lips that continuously praise you for possessing the perfect physique. Once you are dancing, pause and ask yourself this question, did I enjoy this dance, or am I willing to have, "A good man for sale."

WHO IS HE?

I know you have heard about or witnessed firsthand the diverse types of men out there. With that in mind, let's talk. First of all, let me apologize for all the men that have lied about their true motives in hopes of personal gain. These men give men as a whole a bad stigma. There are **married** men, who may feel trapped in a relationship. These men are in a relationship that may have not been well thought out in its inception. I have met men who are in a committed relationship, yet they still feel alone. You may know a man that is **single**, but lacks the self-confidence to pursue a meaningful relationship. You also have those men who choose to be **manipulative** towards unsuspecting women, trapping them into a false sense of hope. I have heard many women ask why men lie to women, and this is what I deciphered. Men who are untruthful about themselves or their relationship status seem to always have an ulterior motive. Be weary of these men, because they will take what they can get at any cost. *Ladies, a man can only take what you give willingly.* Then you have those men who are struggling with their sexuality and are **bisexual**. In many instances these men hid their true sexuality and are known as, 'down low men.' I have spoken to a few of these men and they have shared stories of being molested as a child to being rapped in jail. Out of shame they continued having physical intimacy with unsuspected women to save face. The sad truth is that many sexual transmitted diseases are transmitted between partners.

Many women are so caught up with the idea of being in a relationship that they don't allow themselves time to validate if they have actually established a real one. If you meet a man, and you exchange numbers, you may both go out, you have sex, then what? I have observed women, time after time who have assumed that because a man goes through the motions that his intentions are mutual. Not to be bias, but why don't women who are looking for a meaningful relationship take the time to get to know a man? What is the rush? Don't give me the excuse that your biological clock is ticking, because it has no bearing on finding a man of worth.

Benjamin Franklin said it best, "*Haste makes waste.*"

It has been brought to my attention that women are asking the question, "*How much time should be invested finding out if a man is willing to be totally committed to me?*" To be honest, there is no real time frame, but one should allow enough time to see him at his worst. We all know that when a person is under a tremendous amount of stress, they tend to take off the mask. Then you can make an educated hypothesis of whom you are dealing with: can he still be a perfect gentleman while his whole world is crumbling around him?

Question: Do you know a man of substance, right from the start? The Word says in Matthew 7:20KJV, "*By the fruits of their labor, you shall know them.*" Yes, there are men who are really good at being deceitful, so listen with your mind as opposed to your emotions. Trust me, you'll pick up on their motives. Mankind has discovered over time that following one's heart feels good for the moment, but has catastrophic repercussions. Therefore, we must guide and protect our hearts from deceitful people. In my opinion, it wouldn't hurt to do a background check on him prior to your first date so you can compare his version of his life with the facts.

Women in general, should try to understand that effective communication involves 80% listening and 20% talking. When you first meet a guy, ask open-ended questions on how he perceives himself, then sit back and listen. As simple as it may sound, you can learn a lot. Does he ramble on about himself and his accomplishments? Does he modestly answer and invite you to share? Then ask him about his past and present experience with relationships.

For example, "Are you married?" Then enjoy the awkward pause. Watch his body language, does he look nervous? *Never let on that you know more than he is telling, because you don't want him to be honest out of obligation, as opposed to using his integrity.*

Far too often, I hear of women who wear their hearts on their sleeve and allow their longing to fill an empty void to cloud their reasoning skills. After the first encounter you should be able to have a good feel for the man; so be honest with yourself and don't doubt your gut feeling (it is usually right). Think about the interaction in your mind. Did he stimulate your mind (mental intimacy)? Did he make you laugh? As you spoke to him did he make you feel comfortable in his presence, almost like you've known him? Did he seem like someone who would be sensitive to your needs? During the first encounter you should have picked up on signs, such as him going out of his way to cater to you. Now, let's be honest: just because a man shows an act of kindness doesn't mean he is the one for you, but it is a positive sign.

HIS THOUGHTS

I was reading an article from clinical psychologist Alon Gratch, Ph.D., author of "If Men Could Talk." He shared a valid concept, which states that a man must be 51% in the mindset to settle down, and the remaining 49% is reserved for him to find the right woman. To be totally honest (from a man's perspective), I couldn't agree more. Let's think about it for a moment. In my opinion, a single man in most cases is enjoying life, and really has no concern of catering to a woman emotionally. In fact, he may only have *his* needs in mind, so be careful. He enjoys meeting different women who may fill different voids in his life. Keep in mind that none of these women may actually play any real significant role in his life. I have noticed that many single males have a very carefree outlook as it pertains to relationships, which is natural. These types of men enjoy the moment and are prone to keeping their feelings to a minimum.

CAN YOU IMAGINE?

As a human being we all want to be loved for who we are with all our imperfections. Men truly are peculiar beings, yet they are simple in logic. Can you imagine that men actually have a code of ethics, which clearly states, never attempt to change a harlot into a housewife? Men find it fun to play with a provocative woman in the streets, but most won't dare bring one home. *Yes, I admit, men have the cunning ability to compartmentalize their emotions, which enables them to be physically intimate with a woman without emotional attachment.* So, I guess you could say that, *a man can go through the motions, without emotions.* Yes, I know it's sad, but true. Also, women really should let go of their superstitions about men. For instance: all men are dogs or scared of commitment. *Just because a man refuses to be attached to you does not distinguish if he is a good or bad man.* Far too many times women fall victim to the false pretense that a man wants to be in a committed relationship after a brief sexual encounter. Men are black and white; you might want to question his motives in advance, before you give up more than you bargained for.

Men also have egos, and nothing can kill a man's ego like finding out that every man has had a fair turn at trying out his woman in bed. Now, I know that this doesn't apply to any of the ladies reading this book. If you would, tell your lady friends that a decent man wants a decent (or spiritually sound) woman he can trust and be proud of, no matter where they are. In fact: I am curious as to why there are still women who are attracted to the bad boy image? Women seem to be surprised when the bad boy image ends in heartache and chaos. One might want to reflect on why one is attracted to promiscuous, abusive, criminal minded, lazy or ungodly men. *Most women fail to realize that they have traits similar to the men they attract (hence the laws of attraction).* I believe that women who posses these traits are truly attracted to men who have no zeal to settle down. *Please, don't be fooled into believing that these men are a direct reflection of men as whole, but more so on the individual pursuing them.*

HIS THOUGHTS

Let's be logical (or think like a man), if you want to know what a man desires then just ask. Well, as easy as it may sound, I guess it would make too much sense, right? Ladies, stop wasting your time chasing after the lost cause of trying to manipulate a man. *Please know that there is nothing that you can do or say to make a man love you; he either does or he doesn't.* I have listened to numerous women who have concocted ridiculous superstitions about men. *"Inspiration without information leads to superstition,"* Mutabaruka 2009. This phrase means that there are people who know little about a subject, so they make up assumption to answer their suspicions. I hear many women who claim to strive to make their man happy, when in reality they are catering to their own comforts and then baffled by the man's frustration. In plain English, stop assuming you know what a man wants or needs, just ask him.

JUST REMARKABLE

I pondered the notion, what you see is what you get
Why you ask, because I can't believe you picked me
I am much more than a chiseled frame, meet my sound mind
I have often pondered how one can judge a book by its cover
I have found that words can reveal the heart of a man
A man is more than what is seen, if you look closer
Many of us hide behind our rough exterior in self-defense
We rely on the notion that we are the strong silent type
There are many of us who long to share a thought
There are many who seek mental intimacy
There are many who yearn for love, in its purest form
There are many of us who wish you could see the real man
There are many of us who are weary of searching for a remarkable you
In reality there are only a few that may have the chance to meet you
Now isn't that just remarkable?

NINE

If You Don't, Who Will?

You Do Know Men Have Needs-Right?

"A relationship truly is a selfless component of life that one must be mature in character to initiate and patient enough to maintain."
– Drew L. Hinds 2009

I have a question. If a man has a woman in his life, why would he have to go to a friend's house to get a home cooked meal? Here is another one: if a man has a spouse, why would he have to seek someone else to encourage him before he prepares to speak at his first press conference? Even better: if a man has a significant other why would he have to find someone else to comfort him in his time of bereavement? Well, I know some of you are saying, he doesn't have to find someone else, he chose to. Be honest with yourself: why would a man go outside of his relationship for support when he made a conscious decision to be with you?

A good man should verbalize his concerns to his spouse and not make any rash decisions. If he truly loves his woman, he will be patient and take into consideration that she may have new circumstances that have taken immediate precedence. Such as pregnancy, sudden illnesses, death of a love one, or depression. When a man has made a conscious effort to assist in these circumstances, yet still receives no positive feedback, then there will be an *emotional blockage*. Now, these are just a few reasons (not an excuse), as to why men drift away from home. Women, please don't ever let your friends, jobs, family, finances, profession, or endeavors come between you and the man you love.

BACK TO BASICS

There are many women that have the notion that they deserve a good man, yet they fail to realize that they must put in the necessary work to maintain the merger. When I say *put in work,* I am referring to the act of making the necessary preparation to receive the blessing of having a good man in one's life. *The Word refers to a woman as a helpmate: this implies that she was created to help a man achieve his goals.* If a woman plans on being a wholesome companion, she should continuously attempt to find ways to help her man achieve his true potential. One must understand that a relationship requires a selfless personality.

A self-absorbed person is no use to any one, and should stay out of the dating arena. *Far too many times women overlook the fact that their mates need help, which could become burdensome if the void is left unfulfilled.* Of course, today's media doesn't help; instead it glorifies the power struggle between the sexes. Men as a whole are in need of women who understand their needs, as opposed to just sexual appeal. Men yearn for motivation and the calming qualities that a woman possesses. In this day and age, life can be so overwhelming with day-to-day stresses of life, and relationships are being challenged economically. *Women should keep in mind that there are a lot of other women competing for the same man.* Many other women are also looking for the same thing in a man; so don't take his kindness for weakness. Learn to cherish your mate and in return he will reciprocate the admiration.

STANDBY

I am not sure if women understand that for every time you have a meaningless argument, that there are four ready women who are willing to give aid to your man. *I am referring to women who recognize your man's potential and are willing to cater to his every need.* In fact, these women may also be from a man's past, not only the present. Most men don't go looking for *standby women*; these women make themselves readily available (like a waitress at a local restaurant). I have found that these women tend to want a man who has potential and substance. They are drawn to men who are involved, lonely, defeated, and seemed to have lost hope along the way. These women have been hurt emotionally, and in some cases physically, by past relationships. They see a difference in their newfound male companion. They made bad choices in the past, and they have learned from them. However, they seek to regain a new chance with a willing and capable man who has been neglected as they have.

These women understand how it feels to be lonely within a relationship; therefore, they can empathize with a defeated man. I have learned over time that there are many proud women who have been broken, and as a result, they have become *standby women*. *Don't get me wrong, these women haven't lost respect for themselves; instead, they have gained a new respect for a good man. Standby women* take that newfound respect and use it to fuel their drive to entice a willing man to acknowledge their bare attributes. I have always been fascinated by the process of people having to go through rough times in order for them to appreciate the little things in life.

REFLECTION

Question: Do you really think that most men are miserable by nature? Do you think it is within your power (as a woman), to counteract his moods? Is it wise to ignore a man's moodiness? Could his moodiness be a nonverbal cue? It's funny, now that I think about it, but have you ever noticed that women on a whole seem to know how to persuade a man to do her bidding at will? Yet, it is fascinating that I hear women complaining that they can't get their man out of his moods. Could it be that some women only put forth the effort to cater to a man when she is receiving a fringe benefit?

Trust me, I have witnessed women lose their cool when they don't get their way, and then they focus their frustrations on the man. *Ladies, sometimes I wish you could see and hear yourselves when you are annoyed; it's a wonder that any man has taken a chance with you at all.* Please be mindful that men of all walks of life know the ratio of men to women, and have the comfort of knowing that they will find a replacement after their present relationship ends.

SOLUTION

Please, don't think that I have over looked the fact that you have needs as women; but be honest, women rarely listen to a man's needs as it relates to this emotion. Men need woman to be available to simply listen to their feelings. Yes, he may ramble on; but if he feels that you are truly interested - *then he will allow himself to become vulnerable to your assistance.* Ladies, continuously try to set a positive environment for him to self disclose, free of judgment. All humans thrive on positive reinforcement, so as individuals we must be proactive in our diligence to preserve a meaningful relationship. I am referring to finding a way to have open discussions with your man to find out his likes and dislikes, and then cater to him. Also, find out what's going on with him daily by encouraging open dialogue where he feels relaxed enough to verbalize, what is ailing him.

Yes, I agree that there are many men who have a hard time verbally expressing themselves, but they can still communicate. Ladies, please be optimistic. If a man tells you that he is tired, then he has communicated more than enough. Don't jump to conclusions that he is making an excuse: just take it for what it is. He is expressing that he is mentally, physically, and emotionally exhausted. Now, that may or may not be your fault, so don't take the blame ladies. Just allow him to elaborate at a later date in his own time. Men can be like helpless babies at times, they cry out and you have to cater to them until you find out what's wrong.

It's funny, some men really don't know what's causing their mood swings, and they truly need your help in finding the solution. You will get much further with a man by being patient, don't interrogate him, but be supportive. Some men would label the interrogation process as a form of nagging. If a woman doesn't get the answer she deems correct, then she will drag out the issue until it becomes a national crisis. Now we have a woman who initially set out to help her man relax and release; instead she has provoked him to wrath. This ends in the male half having an emotional meltdown. He then decides to dissolve the relationship with a pack of cigarettes, a bottle of gin, and some old college friends at an adult entertainment center.

DIVORCE

Let me start by saying, if a man wants to leave, then let him go. Ladies, don't make the sad mistake of begging a man to stay in your life when he has his heart and eyes elsewhere. *If you make the mistake of persuading a man who has repeatedly told you he wants out, to stay in your life, then get ready to share your man with another.* Trust me, a man will get what he wants regardless of your consent. You deserve better; so find someone who loves you for you. Far too many times women of all walks of life settle for men who don't appreciate them. You must first love yourself to know what truly makes you happy.

For those who have kids, please seek counseling for them to assist them through the process. Divorce can take quite a toll on adolescents, and they need to be assured that they are not the cause of the divorce. As I child, I remembered feeling that I was the one who caused the divorce, and it bothered me for quite some time. Guard your kids from emotional distress, and you will ensure that next generation will have a positive outlook on life.

CHEATER

I would be doing you a big injustice if I didn't mention this factor. Let me start by disclosing that I don't condone this negative act. *You see different people cheat for different reasons, yet it should not be excused.* No matter the circumstance, don't ever involve yourselves in a negative love triangle. I say that because most parties involved don't consider the revolving door: what goes around comes around. If a man cheats on his present partner, then it is very likely that he will do the same to you. Four out of ten times a person who ventures outside of their relationship is cheating with a person who is aware of their relationship status.

Question: why is it that some women want a man so badly that they are willing to share a man, and settle for being his "*Night Cap*?" This is a woman that is aware that a man is spoken for, but makes herself sexually available. She has overlooked the ramification of her actions to fulfill her immediate void. *If you give it some thought, then you will come to the conclusion that you can't make future plans with a person who has multiple partners.* We should try to sustain from getting involved with someone who is already involved; it just might be to your disadvantage. In fact, it wouldn't be a bad idea to remind these promiscuous males how it would feel on the receiving end of the deception. In conclusion, if a man is interested in you, then let him be free of all ties: past and present.

HIS OPTIONS

I think more women would be more proactive, if they acknowledged the fact that there will always be other women who are willing to cater to their present man. I have heard guys say, "Man, I have had enough of her arguing about everything, I was better off by myself." *It maybe hard to imagine, but there are women who would do anything to be in your shoes and have your trivial issues.* Oh, here is a good one: a woman decides she is upset and she is going to punish her spouse by not engaging in physical intimacy with him. Well, in her mind she has won and is disciplining him, like a trained animal. Wrong, in essence you have turned your domesticated poodle into a hunter (which is his natural instinct).

I urge all women to remember what brought you both together initially, and try to maintain that same spark that initiated the relationship. Men have proven over time that that they are consistent in nature, so keep that in mind when dealing with men in general. Whether conscious or unconscious, a man will give off pheromones, which will alert other women (such as standbys) that he is in need of attention. *Let me just end by saying: a man will always get what he wants (if he wants it bad enough), even without your assistance.* So, with that said, you may want to assist him in his endeavor to find happiness. That is, unless you are willing to have, "A good man for sale."

I NEED YOU

I have a lot on my mind, would you listen?
I had a rough day, can you hold me?
I almost lost it today, can you relate?
I have lost hope, would you pray?
I received some bad news, would you stay?
It really isn't getting any easier, can you love me?

I'm glad I am not alone, its times like this when I need you
Please, know that I need you

TEN

Never Compromise

You Wouldn't Do It, Why Should He?

"We all have learned beliefs and standards of living that shape our character. One shouldn't give up who they are to justify their allegiance to a significant other, they will lose self worth." – Drew L. Hinds 2009

INTIMATE POTLUCK

There is a popular cliché by Senate chaplain the Rev. Peter Marshall in his prayer offered at the opening of the session, April 18, 1947, that says, *"Give to us clear vision that we may know where to stand and what to stand for—because unless we stand for something, we shall fall for anything."* I always ask people to tell me who they are and exactly what do they believe in. You must be true to yourself concerning your likes and dislikes before you can have hopes of successfully engaging in a meaningful relationship. Once you have learned what makes you happy and how to love yourself, I want you to then look at relationship as an *intimate potluck*.

At a typical potluck, everyone brings food to share with others at a designated gathering; and so it should be in a relationship. I am referring to a relationship where both parties are happy as individuals, but choose to share their happiness with one another. Both parties bring support, maturity, diversity, and self-motivation as well compromises to the relationship. These are necessity in maintaining a healthy relationship. Far too many times, there are people who initiate relationships that are empty, insecure, lonely, and broken. There are people who lack true principles to build a solid foundation, and then they wonder why things go wrong. A significant other's motive for embracing should be mutual, positive, and sincere.

KNOW YOU

I have witnessed many people who have initiated a relationship, yet have found themselves unhappy in the process. These individuals didn't appreciate having to comply with their partner's needs. This was due to the fact they realized that they wanted their partner to reciprocate the gesture, but lack the knowledge of what truly made themselves happy. You would be surprised how many individuals never took the time to get know themselves, in relation to discovering their own likes and dislikes. How can a person expect someone else to cater to them if they don't know what makes themselves happy?

You see, because everyone is different, you have to teach others how to love you. *If you leave your likes and dislikes up to another person's assumptions then you are setting your relationship up for failure.* Men love to cater, but you have to teach and reward. This simply means explaining your expectations and then praising them when they comply. Yes, it sounds simple, but I have come across a few women who expect a man to just know how to please them. Ladies, this notion is not realistic. Now, I can understand if you have taught your man about your overall disposition and he is still lost; then you are on your own (it happens). If this is the case, where your partner is obviously not able to cater to you after you have made every provision to assist him, then you may want to rethink investing in him any longer. I often find myself saying, a bad investment can one day be your last investment (just food for thought).

YOUR CHOICE

May I talk to you straight? Do you really think that a man should have to compete with your family, kids, job, friends, past relations, or careers? If so, why? Now, take into consideration that your man has supported you through Grad School, paid off all your credit card debits, and stood by your side after the passing of your parents. Yet still you take his kindness for granted. There are so many women who are alone, but not by choice. Are you puzzled as to why? Well, let's take a closer look at this dilemma. If you put other things before your relationship, then there is no doubt that your relationship will become secondary. One has to seriously prioritize their lives and understand you only get what you put in (cause and effect). There are many other women who are looking for the same qualities in a man that you desire, and in actuality there is a limited supply of good men to go around. Also, you and I know that it is not often you find someone you can truly connect with. So, *when you find that man that moves you mentally as well as emotionally don't take it for granted.* It's a sad notion, that some good women are held captive by their fears that they have lost their one chance for love. Many of us are so scared to give and receive love because of our mental baggage.

THE EXIT

If for any reason you feel like your concerns have been compromised, then verbalize them after you have given them careful thought and revision. It is never a good idea to converse with your significant other, when you are emotionally charged with rage. In some cases, it may be better to write out your thoughts and present it to them in person. Wait for their response, and then you can politely answer their inquiries. This is just one out of many ways to counter act communicating when you feel emotional.

I have learned over the years that it is difficult to let go of someone you have outgrown, mostly because we tend to settle and become complacent. As people, we grow accustomed to negativity, and it becomes our norm. I have said it to you in previous passages: *you must be honest with yourself first, and then you can tackle the challenge of being honest with others.* Walking away from a bad situation isn't a total disaster, but more like liberation (a fresh start). I sometimes compare a breakup to a person who has been driving a vehicle and has gotten into a major car accident. When they finally decide to report it to their insurance, they realize that a brand new car is ready and waiting to replace the broken one.

Like a damaged vehicle, many of us hold on to a broken relationship with hopes that: things will get better, attitudes will change, detrimental habits will cease, deceit would dissipate, and constant disappointment will be a thing of the past. *If you don't remember anything, remember that someone being in your life is a privilege for them, not a right.* Remind yourself, like the damaged vehicle, that you cannot receive a new vehicle in an insurance claim, unless you turn in the old damaged vehicle. Also, you will not be able to give and receive love until you have let go of your hurt and resentment. *Letting go of mental baggage is the key to starting the healing process.*

No, there is no such thing as a perfect relationship. However, a sincere relationship in which two people mutually love and respect each other, and which stimulates mental, spiritual, and physical intimacy, does exist. If you can honestly say to yourself that you have done everything in your capability to remedy the issues to no prevail, then you have finally realized that you deserve to be happy. This is not the end, but your new beginning.

YOUR FAITH

If you are a religious person, there are essential morals that you live by. It is not conducive to compromise your beliefs to accommodate someone you're in love with. *If the person you are involved with has genuine feelings for you, then they will not force you to choose between them and your morals.* I have mentioned this concept earlier in this book, but let me once again touch on being *unequally yoked.* As you know, this describes two individuals who are engaging in a relationship that do not see eye to eye on numerous issues such as: religion, sexuality, child rearing, and finances. Let's be honest; initially when you meet someone, you are so caught up with the visual and audio that you can be easily distracted. There are small details that can ultimately turn into big problems, if overlooked.

Take the time to reevaluate your options, he may just be the one for you. That is, unless you are willing to have, "A good man for sale."

SIMPLY A PRIVILEGE

You are my God, by conviction not confusion.
You are my friend, by choice not by chance.
You are my mentor, by inspiration not eloquence.
You are my love, by value not intimacy.
You are my family, by your untiring dedication not lineage.
You are my employer, by decision not desperation.
You are my associate, by tolerance not status.
It is true, life will go on as it has and as it will.
You are what you are, a privilege to me, not a right.

Final Words

"If it's in your power to help someone, then we as people should never withhold that assistance." –Drew L. Hinds 2008

My true purpose for writing this book was to help woman regain hope in finding the right man that will be good to them. If women would take the time to understand how a man thinks, then it would ease the age-old battle between the sexes. As you and I both know, as a people we tend to fear the unknown, and through time men have been misunderstood. I have come to the understanding that if it's in your power to help someone, then we as people should never withhold that assistance.

I hope that this book has clarified any misconceptions you have had about men, and it has shown the direct effect that lack of intimacy, money, and communication can have on an existing or new relationship. The sooner we identify the root of our relationship issues, the sooner we can hope to rectify them. When you really take a moment and reflect back, it really isn't a mystery how to keep a man, the trick is really finding the right one to invest in. Yes, I did say invest, because if you are truly honest with yourself, that is exactly what it is, an investment. Also, you may want to stop searching for Mr. Right and upgrade to a good man. You see, there is no such thing as a Mr. Right. I say that because every man has faults; but in the end, he just may be good enough for you.

A GOOD MAN FOR SALE

Whether you are looking for a good man, or attempting to keep one, don't allow insecurities to keep you from succeeding in your endeavor to obtain true love. You would be surprised how many ready and willing men are out there. These men are awaiting a woman who can see and appreciate their true potential. If we are honest with ourselves, we can recall being neglected, or in contrast, taking someone else for granted for whatever reason. I guess one could say, that if you truly think that a person would continually deal with your disregard for their well-being, then you are truly making a sad mistake. Everyone desires to be loved, respected, and appreciated; so it would behoove us to emulate these aspects within our daily interactions with the potential love of our lives.

I am starting to value life more and more each day, because life is too short and precious to take for granted. *Honestly, we all need to change our outlook on life; it's not about finding the right person as much as it is becoming the right person.* As humans, we have the ability to attract and repel negative and positive energies, so be mindful of what you are portraying on a daily bases. It would help to focus on the good things in our life, as opposed to all the bad things that you have encountered. For many of us, a sound relationship is just around the corner, so we all need to be prepared to receive it as a true blessing. In my younger days, I recall hearing the cliché, "If you can believe it, then you can achieve it." I truly believe it now more than ever.

For the record, a good man is out there for every woman, and when you meet him, you will know that he is worth holding on to. You may want to stop setting unrealistic expectations that you expect men to live up to; especially when you can't seem to live up to those same standards. I urge you to search for a man with your mind first, and then use your heart to test his true worth. I also challenge you to become a better person first and see how much easier it is to attract and retain your equal. That is, unless you are willing to have yet another, "Good man for sale."

This is a 2011 interview of Drew L. Hinds by Author Deborah Cofer, prior to the release of this book:

Introduction: As an author, women's health educator, inspirational speaker and last...but not least, a seasoned woman, mother and grandmother, I often speak with women who have more questions than answers to how they can achieve and enhance their romantic relationships. While I've written a relationship book that provides them with information I designed to provide some greater insight on living, loving, learning and letting go...from a woman's perspective, I believe that hearing from men who possess the level of understanding and spiritual wisdom required to Xpound, from a man's perspective, is vital to helping all women gain a wholesome as well as a more balanced understanding of how men think and feel. Women open up to each other, but connecting to and hearing from men who are able to do the same provides awesome nourishment for minds in search of answers and hearts in need of healing. So, in an effort to provide the caliber of connection I think women need to gain a clearer understanding about how a man thinks, feels and what his needs are, I decided to ask a literary colleague and friend, Drew Hinds...author of "Don't Spoil Your Appetite" and "A Good Man For Sale" to share his thoughts on what, I believe, are important questions and answers on the topic of love and romance. His responses are honest and will take those who 1) take the time to meditate on his answers, 2) thoroughly digest the knowledge provided and 3) receive the wisdom that's coming straight from his heart, to new levels of awareness and relationship success. Read, take your time and take heed. What you are about to receive will definitely feed your soul, energize your spirit and help you develop a winning formula for creating the relationship you desire, deserve and were born to fully Xperience:

Question #1: How do you define love? Is it a set of attributes? Is it a feeling…or is it both?

Response: Let's see, I would say that love is broken into two parts, emotional & principle. I think that, for the most part, we all are familiar with that warm and fuzzy feeling that makes us feel as though we can't imagine ourselves without that person we deem "special" in our lives (in fact it hurts to fathom life without them). On the other hand, love the principle is about doing, even when it hurts. And even though we may not be pleased with the other person's decisions or choices we choose to lovingly care for them unconditionally.

Question #2: People often say that they "fell in love." Do you think that there is a difference between "falling in love" and "growing in love?" If so, can you elaborate?

Response: It's funny you should ask. From my perspective most of the women I know, fall in love. I am referring to the act of experiencing an emotional attachment to someone they barely know, without a guarantee of receiving what they define as "love" in return. Men, on the other hand, are logical creatures who need to see consistency over a period of time. In essence, men are more prone to "grow in love" with a woman. When it comes to love, I find that men are a lot more conditional than women; but when it comes to emotional security I think that both men and women are pretty equal in their need to feel safe and secure in whatever romantic relationship they ultimately establish.

Question #3: What are your thoughts on the "Mr. Right" mindset that so many women embrace? Do you think their Xpectations are realistic or are their perceptions of "Mr. Right" based, mostly, on their own insecurities and lack of interpersonal relationship intelligence?

Response: To be honest I believe that the concept of "Mr. Right" is not an invalid mindset at all. Our God and Creator, in His infinite wisdom, said "It is not good for man to be alone." In that moment, man was given a woman that was formed and fashioned from his rib, which symbolically represents the depths of the bond that is supposed to exist between two people who come together "in God's name." To take this point a little deeper, I believe that the rib analogy also signifies that a man is not complete without a woman. She is the missing portion of a man and, hence, is his soul-mate. Now don't get me wrong, what may be right for one woman may be wrong for another. The famous cliché, "One man's trash is another man's treasure" definitely applies from one person to another. One man is not designed to complete or please all women. This is the privilege of the one who completes him and comforts him in ways no other woman can. He is her "Mr. Right," and she is his "Ms. Right."

Question #4: How long did you and your wife, Sandy date before you knew she your "Ms. Right?"

Response: I'm not sure, we were associates and one day we decided to spend more time quality time together. She allowed me to be in her space, her family, her heart, her hopes, her dreams, her vision, her womb, her life, and I love her for that. I firmly believe that an intimate/romantic relationship is not an entitlement; it is a privilege we must each earn.

Question #5: What do you believe are the most important aspects of relationships that both women and men need to gain a better understanding of?

Response: I've always expressed that clear communication is the most important aspect of a wholesome relationship. We have to first understand that all interpersonal-communication consists of 80% listening and 20% talking. And unfortunately men, by nature, are not known for our skill when it comes to listening and understanding a woman's needs. This is a big reason why there are more relationship disasters than successes. On the other hand, women need to gain a better understanding that they must learn to be more patient and lead by example. This means that they need to engage in less lip-service and more action. Women must teach men the importance of listening, by setting the caliber of example that is required to firmly establish the both the logic and value of "listening." When this is done, the reciprocity of two people's interaction helps to create balance that, in turn, produces the caliber of results they want, and need, to establish relationship longevity.

Question #6: What do you think are the reasons so many people drastically miss the mark when it comes to establishing and maintaining the caliber of relationship they profess to want?

Response: Plain and simple they come into relationships with hidden agendas that are more self-centered in nature. For example, a woman may get into a relationship to live what she considers to be "the good life" or to have a baby. On the other-hand the man is with her for her curves or external beauty (not to say that men are shallow like that... LOL). In each of these simple examples, there is a problem. If the woman gets her child from the relationship, but didn't come to a general consensus with the man, he can become resentful and, consequently, not much more than a whole lot of baby's momma's drama is produced...(sigh). And the man may get the trophy he wants, but behind the trophy is a materialistic female who ultimately becomes nothing more than a shallow reflection of two lost souls who just don't get it. I also believe it is important to stress that being "clueless" is a mental disease not an excusefor being ignorant. We must express our honest intentions from the beginning; and continuously do so in order to solidify the "till death do we part" statement made during our wedding vows.

Question #7: Do you agree with author, John Gray's concept that "Men Are From Mars and Women Are From Venus?" Is there really that much of a difference and distance in how men and women think? If so, how can we bridge the gap?

Response: Good question; are men and women really that much different? I would say, no. Both require love and affection, a sense of belonging, emotional security, and feed on the inherent need to give and receive love. I think the distance is created as a result of how both sexes go about getting their needs met. For example, a woman may resort to nagging a man for attention, yet a man may get moody and become withdrawn if his needs are not met. These unfulfilling outcomes can all be remedied through good-old-fashion conversation. Again, acquiring good interpersonal communication skills is a life-skill that maximizes both the quality and longevity of our relationships.

Question #8: In what ways do you think television shows like Housewives of Atlanta and New Jersey impact on the realities of marriage?

Response: How does reality-television impact on the realities of marriage? Wow, this is definitely a profound and relative question in today's media-driven society. I have observed that women have become more demanding and materialistic and men have become more possessive and less considerate. Movies, television and talk-shows promote and support so many immoral beliefs and behaviors that, in my opinion, are detrimental to the development and positive growth of relationships, families, communities, mental-wellness and society as a whole. Most people have become desensitized to violence and crime as well as far too complacent of the sexually explicit marketing that drives every aspect of the marketing process. Our children are out of control and divorce is at an all-time high. Television, as well as many other marketing mediums, have and continue to negatively impact on the psyches of the average consumer of shows I think can be considered more garbage for the minds of the psychically unstable than reality for those seeking truth and positive direction! Need I say more?

Question #9: Why is it that Black men have a reputation for being untrustworthy with their women? Do you believe that their distrust is based on legitimate reasons? What do you think can be done to turn this situation around?

Response: Black men have a reputation of being untrustworthy with their woman, because of the following reasons: lack of communication, self-centered ulterior motives, repetitive media distortions and deceptions. As I mentioned earlier, good communication skills are paramount to the process of understanding how to communicate with Black women in America who, for the most part, have carried the cross of pain, suffering and struggle of the Black family faithfully for more years than most people care to remember. And in alignment with civil rights activist Fannie Lou Hamer they have grown way beyond being "sick and tired of being sick and tired." It is important for Black men to humbly acknowledge and accept this fact, and step up to the plate when it comes to the state of confusion and collapses that currently exists within our relationships and family units. Far too many Black men are not taking full responsibility for the babies they make, the women they hurt and the negative perceptions they continue to create within the minds of Black women. In reality, many Black men have earned the distrust they are experiencing and must take responsibility for rectifying the damage they have done. I also talked about "motives" in one of the previous questions. There needs to be honest dialog about the intentions and capabilities of both parties who are coming together, as a couple, or retaliation (cheating) and dislike for one another will continue to be the byproduct of their immaturity or blatant refusal to be both realistic and honest. Last but not least, the media portrayals of Black men have been more negative than positive. From the beginning of America's history we have witness how Black-Americans (especially Black men), have been inaccurately portrayed as less than human or nothing more than sexual vultures. I have come to the belief that we, as a people, need to recognize that it is not what we are called or how we are perceived by others that matters most, what we believe about ourselves has much greater value. We have hung our heads in shame, bleached our skin, processed our hair and starved ourselves from food, knowledge and wisdom to the point of total starvation. God is our rock. But the Black man is and must take his rightful place as the source of strength through which God is able to return us to our rightful place as the true source for the survival and enhancement of our family units. In turn, it is the responsibility of the Black Woman to recognize when she is dealing with a so-called man who lacks the caliber of honor it takes to be the "head" of the family rather than the butt of stereotypical jokes. White America is not the Black Man and Black Woman's savior and is not responsible for our salvation. Today and every day, as we continue to grow and evolve in powerful ways, we must take full rather than partial responsibility for our choices, failures and successes. This is what ultimately defines whether or not any Black male has achieved the level of maturity that truly defines him as a "man."

Question #10: How important do you think loyalty is in a relationship?

Response: Loyalty definitely adds the extra sugar and spice and everything nice to the process of creating, strengthening and enhancing a relationship. I understand that women, in general want honesty, but if the truth be told most men are scared of being left feeling vulnerable and emasculated. Believe it or not, there are women who use a man's honesty as a weapon against him. As a result there are wounded and broken men, who drag around mental baggage from past relationships, who fear allowing any woman to see into their souls. And consequently, won't share at all. This same scenario also holds true for women. But, make no mistake no-one should be, for any reason at any time, subjected to misused confessions. We all need to find a way to reestablish the loyalty factor. This act of love powers up the kindness that's needed to ensure and continuously strengthen the caliber of relationship-bonds that is unshakable, unbreakable and unforgettable.

Conclusion: WOW…these are all Words of Wisdom that I strongly believe will help many women to recognize and begin the task of identifying and Xing-out the negative beliefs and negative behaviors that block the path to healthy, happy and heavenly relationship Xperiences. Drew, I have always admired your openness, honesty and efforts to empower others; but your responses have helped me to gain an even deeper awareness of what a truly open, honest, awesome and got-it-going on man you really are. Thank you for being so candid! The only thing left to say is to you…the reader. Drew and I have done our parts. Now, it's your turn to Xtract the information you deem valuable to strengthen your plan to establish, build, nourish, strengthen, and enhance the kind of relationship you have always wanted, without losing a large chunk of your self-esteem in the process! - **Deborah Cofer 2011**

www.ingramcontent.com/pod-product-compliance
Lightning Source LLC
Chambersburg PA
CBHW050654160426
43194CB00010B/1929